Bosworth v. Continental Illinois Bank & Trust Co. U.S. Supreme Court Transcript of Record with Supporting Pleadings

SIDNEY S GORHAM, ISAAC H MAYER, Additional Contributors

Bosworth v. Continental Illinois Bank & Trust Co.
Petition / SIDNEY S GORHAM / 1933 / 358 / 290 U.S. 621 / 54 S.Ct. 207 / 78 L.Ed. 542 / 8-18-1933
Bosworth v. Continental Illinois Bank & Trust Co.
Brief in Opposition (P) / ISAAC H MAYER / 1933 / 358 / 290 U.S. 621 / 54 S.Ct. 207 / 78 L.Ed. 542 / 9-11-1933
Bosworth v. Continental Illinois Bank & Trust Co.
Transcript of Record / U.S. Supreme Court / 1933 / 358 / 290 U.S. 621 / 54 S.Ct. 207 / 78 L.Ed. 542 / 8-18-1933
Bosworth v. Continental Illinois Bank & Trust Co.
Petitioner's Brief / F G AWALT / 1933 / 358 / 290 U.S. 621 / 54 S.Ct. 207 / 78 L.Ed. 542 / 1-11-1934
Bosworth v. Continental Illinois Bank & Trust Co.
Respondent's Brief / ISAAC H MAYER / 1933 / 358 / 290 U.S. 621 / 54 S.Ct. 207 / 78 L.Ed. 542 / 2-5-1934
Bosworth v. Continental Illinois Bank & Trust Co.
Reply Brief / F G AWALT / 1933 / 358 / 290 U.S. 621 / 54 S.Ct. 207 / 78 L.Ed. 542 / 2-7-1934

Bosworth v. Continental Illinois Bank & Trust Co. U.S. Supreme Court Transcript of Record with Supporting Pleadings

Table of Contents

IN THE

Supreme Court of the United States

OCTOBER TERM, A. D. 1933.

No. 358

L. J. BOSWORTH, RECEIVER OF THE McCARTNEY NATIONAL
BANK OF GREEN BAY, WISCONSIN.

Petitioner,

vs.

CONTINENTAL ILLINOIS BANK AND TRUST
COMPANY,

Respondent.

PETITION FOR WRIT OF CERTIORARI AND PETITIONER'S BRIEF.

AMOS C. MILLER,
Counsel for Petitioner.

SIDNEY S. GORHAM,
HENRY W. WALES,
EDWARD R. ADAMS,
Of Counsel.

THE GUNTHORP-WARREN PRINTING COMPANY, 210 WEST JACKSON, CHICAGO

INDEX.

Supreme Court of the United States

OCTOBER TERM, 1933.

No. ....

L. J. BOSWORTH, RECEIVER OF THE McCARTNEY NA-
TIONAL BANK OF GREEN BAY, WISCONSIN,

Petitioner,

vs.

CONTINENTAL ILLINOIS BANK AND TRUST
COMPANY,

Respondent.

PETITION FOR A WRIT OF CERTIORARI TO THE UNITED STATES CIRCUIT COURT OF APPEALS FOR THE SEVENTH CIRCUIT.

L. J. Bosworth, Receiver of the McCartney National Bank of Green Bay, Wisconsin, at the direction of the Comptroller of the Currency of the United States, prays that a writ of certiorari issue to review the judgment of the Circuit Court of Appeals for the Seventh Circuit entered June 5, 1933. The jurisdiction of this Court is invoked under Section 240 (a) of the Judicial Code as amended by the Act of February 13, 1925.

QUESTION PRESENTED.

Whether in a suit by the receiver of an insolvent national bank to recover a deposit balance, the defendant may set off collection items, drawn on said insolvent bank, not beneficially owned by the defendant.

STATEMENT.

This action was brought by L. J. Bosworth, as Receiver of an insolvent national bank, to recover the amount on deposit with the respondent bank to the credit of the insolvent bank. The respondent (defendant below) resisted the action on the ground that it had the right to set off against the amount of the deposit a sum representing the amount of certain checks forwarded by the respondent to the insolvent bank prior to its closing. The case was heard on two stipulations of fact and a very small amount of additional testimony introduced by the respondent. The trial court, sitting without a jury, allowed the set-off and entered judgment for the defendant. (R. 21; Memorandum Opinion, R. 14.) The Circuit Court of Appeals for the Seventh Circuit affirmed the judgment. (R. 58; Opinion, R. 54, reported 65 F. (2) 632.)

The set-off claimed by the respondent is alleged to have arisen by reason of certain checks it held for collection and forwarded to The McCartney National Bank. These checks drawn on The McCartney National Bank were delivered to the respondent by its depositors under a written agreement expressly providing, among other things, that the respondent "acts only as depositor's collecting agent and assumes no responsibility beyond the exercise of due care. All items are credited or cashed subject to final payment in cash or solvent credits." (R. 25.) The respondent credited its respective depositors for the amounts of these checks (R. 23), but there were no withdrawals against these credits, nor any existing overdrafts in the respective customers' accounts before the respondent charged the amounts back against its customers, as set forth below. (R. 26.)

The respondent forwarded these checks to The McCartney National Bank on May 26, 1931, for collection and returns in Chicago Exchange. (R. 23.) The following day The McCartney National Bank received the checks, charged them to the respective accounts of its customers who had issued them, and mailed to the respondent its draft on the Federal Reserve Bank of Chicago for the total amount of the checks. (R. 23.)

That evening, May 27, 1931, the Directors of The McCartney National Bank adopted a resolution closing the bank, and the bank failed to open for business on the following morning. A representative of the Comptroller of the Currency took charge of the bank on the morning of May 28, 1931. (R. 23.) On the morning of May 28, 1931, the respondent received the draft sent it by The McCartney National Bank and presented it to the Federal Reserve Bank of Chicago before 10:30 A. M., but payment was refused since prior to the presentation of the draft the Federal Reserve Bank of Chicago had been notified of the closing of The McCartney National Bank. (R. 24.) At 11:15 that same morning the respondent was notified by telegram that The McCartney National Bank had suspended. Thereafter, the respondent charged the deposit account of The McCartney National Bank with the amount of the checks which had been forwarded. However, on May 29th and following days the respondent charged back to the accounts of its customers the amounts of the checks on The McCartney National Bank which had been deposited by them, respectively, and notified its customers of this action. (R. 26.)

At the trial the respondent introduced testimony over the objection of the petitioner that the checks so forwarded to The McCartney National Bank were endorsed "Pay to the order of Continental Illinois Bank and Trust Company," or "Pay to the order of any bank, banker or trust company." (R. 29.)

By agreed adjustment of the accounts petitioner is entitled to recover the sum of $5,890.79, together with interest thereon, if allowable by law, unless the respondent is entitled to set off the amount of the checks forwarded under the above circumstances.

SPECIFICATION OF ERRORS.

1. The Court erred in holding that the defendant might set off an amount not beneficially owned by it against the amount owed by it to the plaintiff, by reason of the deposit of the McCartney National Bank in the defendant.

2. The Court erred in holding that ownership of the collection items involved passed to the defendant sufficiently to allow a set-off.

3. The Court erred in allowing the defendant to set off the amount of the collection items involved.

4. The Court erred in holding that the allowance of the set-off did not result in an unlawful preference to the defendant's customers, as owners of the collection items involved.

5. The Court erred in affirming the judgment for the defendant.

REASONS FOR THE ALLOWANCE OF THE WRIT.

This Court has granted certiorari in the case of *Dakin, Receiver, v. Bayly, Liquidator*, No. 930, in the October Term, 1932. The decision in that case involves the same question presented by the present case, namely, whether a set-off may be allowed of items forwarded for collection against a sum owed by the forwarder in a different capacity. The question, in other words, is whether to create a set-off the debts and credits must be mutual in the sense that they are beneficially owned by the same person. The facts are slightly different in the Dakin case, in that there both banks were acting in the capacity of agents for collection, whereas in the instant case only the respondent was an agent for collection and is attempting to set off the amount of such collection items against an amount individually owed by it. Although there is this slight variation in the facts of the two cases, the principles involved are the same. All the reasons for granting certiorari in the Dakin case are present here, with the additional reason that the rights of the petitioner should be preserved pending the decision of this Court on the question of the allowance of such set-offs.

The petitioner submits that the decisions of this Court require mutuality in the sense that the debts and credits must be beneficially owned in the same capacity before there can be a right of set-off. *Scott* v. *Armstrong*, 146 U. S. 499; *Libby* v. *Hopkins*, 104 U. S. 303; *Scammon* v. *Kimball*, 92 U. S. 362; *U. S.* v. *Butterworth-Judson Corp.*, 267 U. S. 387.

The decision of the District Court in the instant case rested on the proposition that set-off is allowable if the party asserting the right might sue on the claim in his own name. This reasoning substitutes an artificial rule of thumb for the sound principle laid down by this Court requiring that the cross demands be held in the same capacity. The Circuit Court of Appeals in affirming the District Court rested its decision apparently on a sort of qualified ownership acquired by an agent for collection. Even if it could be admitted that any kind of ownership passed to a bank which received a negotiable instrument under an express agreement that it "acts only as the depositors' collecting agent" and "all items are credited or cashed subject to final payment in cash

or solvent credits,'' it is obvious that no *beneficial* ownership passes to the bank under such an arrangement. The
bank suffers no pecuniary loss if the collection is not
made or if the set-off is denied. The allowance of the
set-off creates an unlawful preference. We submit that
both courts have decided an important question of general law in a way probably in conflict with the applicable
decisions of this Court.

There is the further ground for granting certiorari
in the instant case that the decisions of the Circuit Courts
of Appeals of the various Circuits are in conflict. The
Seventh Circuit has decided in the instant case, as did
the Fifth Circuit in *Anderson v. Bayly*, 63 Fed. (2d) 592
(1933) (pending in this Court as *Dakin v. Bayly, supra*),
that the amount of items forwarded for collection are
available for set-off. On the other hand, the reasoning
in *Nomland, Receiver, v. First National Bank*, 64
F. (2d) 399 (1933), indicates that the Eighth Circuit
considers such a set-off not allowable. The set-off in the
Nomland case was allowed solely because the bank forwarding the items had purchased them and had become
the beneficial owners of them in accordance with a contract between the bank and its customers. The earlier
decision of the Eighth Circuit in *Hirning v. Federal Reserve Bank of Minneapolis*, 52 Fed. (2d) 382
(1931), makes it even more clear that in that circuit
such set-offs of collection items are not allowed. Also
in the Fourth Circuit the decision in *Federal Reserve
Bank of Richmond v. Early*, 30 Fed. (2d) 198 (1929),
affirmed on a different point in 281 U. S. 84, held that
where there was no special agreement (as in the cash
surrender value of the Reserve Bank's stock involved in
that case), a set-off may not be allowed of amounts held
in a collection capacity.

The question of set-off is of great importance in the administration of the affairs of insolvent national banks. One of the frequent situations which arises is the one here presented of items which have been forwarded for collection. The principle involved of whether debts to be the subject of set-off must be beneficially owned by the same parties in the same right has an even broader application. The importance of the question in the liquidation of insolvent national banks is apparent from the brief of the Comptroller of the Currency as *amicus curiae* in the case of *Dakin* v. *Bayly*, No. 930, of the October Term, 1932, of this Court. The instant case presents the question in a clear, well-defined manner in the stipulations of fact entered into by the parties. It is for this reason that the Comptroller of the Currency has directed the Receiver to present this petition in the hope that this case may be considered at the same time as the Dakin case. If that is not possible, we submit that certiorari should be granted to preserve the rights of the Receiver in the instant case pending the Dakin decision.

WHEREFORE it is respectfully submitted that the petition for a writ of certiorari be granted to review the judgment of the Circuit Court of Appeals for the Seventh Circuit.

AMOS C. MILLER,
Counsel for Petitioner.

PETITIONER'S BRIEF AND ARGUMENT.

THE DEBTS ARE NOT MUTUAL AND THEREFORE THE SET-OFF IS IMPROPER.

The contract under which the respondent received the items forwarded expressly negatives a purchase—words could not make the relationship of collecting agent clearer. (R. 25.) The District Court recognized that the respondent did not become the owner of the items but was merely agent for collection. (R. 15.) The decision of the Circuit Court of Appeals is less clear on this point, but seems to recognize that as between the respondent and its customers the relationship was only that of collecting agent, indicating that it was no concern of the petitioner what the exact relationship between the respondent and its customers was. Whatever the views of the courts below on this question, there is ample authority to sustain the position that under an express contract such as was present in the instant case, no beneficial ownership passed to the respondent bank. *Kane* v. *First National Bank of El Paso, Tex.*, 56 F. (2d) 534 (C. C. A. 5th, 1932); *Washington Loan & Banking Co.* v. *Fourth National Bank of Macon*, 38 F. (2d) 772 (C. C. A. 5th, 1930); *First National Bank of Denver* v. *Federal Reserve Bank*, 6 F. (2d) 339 (C. C. A. 8th, 1925). Whatever rights the respondent had to sue on the items to effect the collection were subject to the paramount rights of its depositors who remained the owners. The respondent then was acting as collecting agent only, which is exactly what its contract with its customers called for.

A trustee may not set off against a debt owed in an individual capacity one owed him in a fiduciary capacity. *Libby* v. *Hopkins*, 104 U. S. 303; *Hanover National Bank*

9

v. *Suddath,* 215 U. S. 122. These cases show that this is true even in cases of constructive trust where it is merely the beneficial ownership of the respective demands that is looked to. The principle has been applied where the debt owed one party was beneficially owned by his creditors. *Scammon* v. *Kimball,* 92 U. S. 362. We submit that this court has ever since *Scott* v. *Armstrong,* 146 U. S. 499, adhered to the principle that to allow set-off the debts must be mutual in the sense that they are beneficially owned by the respective parties.

At least two circuits have so understood the law with regard to set-off of collection items such as those involved in the instant case. The fourth circuit in *Federal Reserve Bank of Richmond* v. *Early,* 30 F. (2d) 198, 202 (1929), stated:

> "Even in the absence of a statutory direction as to how the liability should be applied, a set-off of checks held for collection against such a liability would not be allowed, for the reason that demands to be set off against each other must be mutual; that is, they must be due to and from the same parties and in the same capacity."

A similar doctrine was followed in *Hirning* v. *Federal Reserve Bank of Minneapolis, Minn.,* 52 F. (2d) 382 (C. C. A. 8th, 1931).

It may also be noted that the decision of the seventh circuit in the instant case allowed a preference to the owners of the items, customers of the respondent. The National Bank Act makes provision for the ratable distribution of the assets of insolvent banks. 12 U. S. C. § 91, 192, 194. Since the assets of the McCartney National Bank were not augmented, the payment in full (or nearly so) of respondent's customers and the resulting preference is improper. *Larrabee Flour Mills* v. *First Nat. Bank of Henryetta, Okla.,* 13 F. (2d) 330 (C. C. A. 8th, 1926), cert. denied 273 U. S. 727; *Ellerbe*

v. *Studebaker Corp. of America*, 21 F. (2d) 993 (C. C. A. 4th, 1927). The fortuitous circumstance that the collecting agent selected was itself indebted to the McCartney National Bank should not affect the result.

CONCLUSION.

The Comptroller of the Currency has directed the filing of this petition for certiorari as important in the administration of the affairs of the national banks. As appears from the brief of the Comptroller in *Dakin* v. *Bayly*, No. 930, October 1932 Term, more than two thousand banks are in the hands of receivers or conservators, and the set-off question is an important one constantly arising. The principles involved in the Dakin case, in which certiorari has been granted, are also presented in the instant case in a little more clear-cut form. Since the Court has determined to pass on the question (presumably by reason of its importance and the conflict of decisions in the various circuits), the Comptroller desires that review be granted in the instant case so that the rights may be preserved and the case may be heard if possible at the same time as the Dakin case.

Respectfuly submitted,

AMOS C. MILLER,
Counsel for Petitioner.

SIDNEY S. GORHAM,
HENRY W. WALES,
EDWARD R .ADAMS,
Of Counsel.

IN THE

Supreme Court of the United States

OCTOBER TERM, A. D. 1933.

No. 358

L. J. BOSWORTH, RECEIVER OF THE MCCARTNEY NATIONAL
BANK OF GREEN BAY, WISCONSIN,

Petitioner,

vs.

CONTINENTAL ILLINOIS BANK AND TRUST
COMPANY,

Respondent.

RESPONDENT'S WAIVER OF RIGHT TO FILE BRIEF IN
OPPOSITION TO PETITION FOR WRIT OF CERTIORARI.

ISAAC H. MAYER,
CARL MEYER,
DAVID F. ROSENTHAL,
FRANK D. MAYER,
Counsel for Respondent.

THE GUNTHORP-WARREN PRINTING COMPANY, 210 WEST JACKSON, CHICAGO

No. 358.

L. J. BOSWORTH, RECEIVER OF THE MCCARTNEY NATIONAL BANK OF GREEN BAY, WISCONSIN,
Petitioner,

vs.

CONTINENTAL ILLINOIS BANK AND TRUST COMPANY,
Respondent.

RESPONDENT'S WAIVER OF RIGHT TO FILE BRIEF IN OPPOSITION TO PETITION FOR WRIT OF CERTIORARI.

Respondent, although convinced of the correctness of the decision of the court below sought to be reviewed, hereby waives its right to file a brief in opposition to the petition for certiorari because (first), this Court has granted certiorari in *Dakin, Receiver v. Bayly, Liquidator,* No. 930 (October Term, 1932) involving the same question as does this case, and (second) the respondent believes that the question is of such importance in the administration of the affairs of insolvent banks that it should be finally determined by this Court.

ISAAC H. MAYER,
CARL MEYER,
DAVID F. ROSENTHAL,
FRANK D. MAYER,
Counsel for Respondent.

TRANSCRIPT OF RECORD

Supreme Court of the United States

OCTOBER TERM, 1933

No. 358

L. J. BOSWORTH, RECEIVER OF THE McCARTNEY
NATIONAL BANK OF GREEN BAY, WISCONSIN,
PETITIONER,

vs.

CONTINENTAL ILLINOIS BANK AND TRUST
COMPANY

ON WRIT OF CERTIORARI TO THE UNITED STATES CIRCUIT
COURT OF APPEALS FOR THE SEVENTH CIRCUIT

PETITION FOR CERTIORARI FILED AUGUST 18, 1933

CERTIORARI GRANTED DECEMBER 4, 1933

SUPREME COURT OF THE UNITED STATES

OCTOBER TERM, 1933

No. 358

L. J. BOSWORTH, RECEIVER OF THE McCARTNEY
NATIONAL BANK OF GREEN BAY, WISCONSIN,
PETITIONER,

vs.

CONTINENTAL ILLINOIS BANK AND TRUST
COMPANY

ON WRIT OF CERTIORARI TO THE UNITED STATES CIRCUIT
COURT OF APPEALS FOR THE SEVENTH CIRCUIT

INDEX

JUDD & DETWEILER (INC.), PRINTERS, WASHINGTON, D. C., DECEMBER 13, 1933

1   Pleas in the District Court of the United States for the Northern District of Illinois, Eastern Division, begun and held at the United States Court Room, in the City of Chicago, in said District and Division, before the Honorable Walter C. Lindley, District Judge of the United States for the Northern District of Illinois on Sixth day of August, in the year of our Lord one thousand nine hundred and Thirty-Two, being one of the days of the regular July Term of said Court, begun Monday, the Fourth day of July, and of our Independence the 157th year.

Present:

Honorable Walter C. Lindley

H. C. W. Laubenheimer, U. S. Marshal.

Charles M. Bates, Clerk.

2   IN THE DISTRICT COURT OF THE UNITED STATES

Northern District of Illinois

Eastern Division

L. J. Bosworth, Receiver of The McCartney National Bank of Green Bay, Wisconsin,
            vs.
Continental Illinois Bank and Trust Company, of Chicago, Illinois.
} No. 40116.

Be It Remembered, that the above-entitled action was commenced by the filing of the following Declaration in the above-entitled cause in the office of the Clerk of the District Court of the United States for the Northern District of Illinois, Eastern Division, on this the 24th day of November, 1931.

3   *   *   (Caption)   *   *

DECLARATION.

L. J. Bosworth, Receiver of The McCartney National Bank
of Green Bay, Wisconsin, plaintiff, by Miller, Gorham and
Wales, his attorneys, complains of Contituental Illinois Bank
and Trust Company, of Chicago, Illinois, defendant, of a plea
of trespass on the case on promises.

First Count.

Plaintiff avers that the matter in controversy exceeds, exclusive of interest and costs, the sum and value of Three
Thousand ($3,000.) Dollars, and is between citizens of dif-
ferent states; that the defendant now is and at all times complained of was a corporation organized under the banking
laws of the State of Illinois and conducting a general
4 banking business in Chicago, Illinois; that The McCartney National Bank now is and at all times complained of
was a corporation organized under the banking laws of the
United States of America and prior to the closing of said
Bank as hereinafter set forth, conducted a general banking
business in Green Bay, Wisconsin.

Plaintiff further avers that this suit is one arising under
Section 41 (16) of Title 28 of the United States Code.

Plaintiff further avers that on the evening of May 27, 1931,
the Directors of The McCartney National Bank adopted a
resolution closing said Bank, and that said The McCartney
National Bank failed to open for business on the morning of
May 28, 1931; that on said 28th day of May, 1931, the affairs of said Bank were surrendered to and taken in charge
by the Comptroller of the Currency through his representative, Harry W. Walker, a National Bank Examiner; that on
the 29th day of May, 1931 plaintiff was duly appointed as
Receiver of The McCartney National Bank by the Comptroller of the Currency; that he duly qualified as such Receiver
and that since said 29th day of May, 1931 plaintiff has been
and now is the acting Receiver of said The McCartney National Bank, and since said date has had possession of all the
books, records and assets of every description of said The
McCartney National Bank.

Plaintiff further avers that for some time prior to May 28, 1931 The McCartney National Bank had and main-
5 tained with defendant a deposit account; that at the opening of business on said 28th day of May, 1931, and before said defendant bank had any notice of the closing of The McCartney National Bank, said defendant had a balance in said deposit account to the credit of The McCartney National Bank of Six Thousand Three and 41/100 ($6,003.-41) Dollars; that subsequently, on said May 28, 1931 and before the defendant bank had any notice of the closing of The McCartney National Bank, deposits aggregating Five Thousand Three Hundred Ninety-eight and 14/100 ($5,398.14) Dollars were credited to said The McCartney National Bank in said deposit account, and withdrawals aggregating Four Hundred Four and 70/100 ($404.70) Dollars were debited to said accounut of The McCartney National Bank, leaving a credit balance in favor of The McCartney National Bank at the time that the defendant received notice of the closing of The McCartney National Bank of Ten Thousand Nine Hundred Ninety-seven and 12/100 ($10,997.12) Dollars.

Plaintiff further avers that subsequent to May 28, 1931 items for which said The McCartney National Bank had received credit from the defendant in its, said The McCartney National Bank's deposit account were returned to defendant unpaid and that said items were charged by defendant to The McCartney National Bank in its said deposit account, thereby reducing said balance to the credit of The McCartney National Bank to Ten Thousand Forty-two and 39/100.
($10,042.39) Dollars; that there was included in said
6 credit balance of Ten Thousand Forty-two and 39/100
($10,042.39) Dollars the sum of Five Hundred Fifteen ($515.) Dollars, representing a bond and coupon collection, which last named amount was subsequently paid over by defendant to plaintiff as Receiver of The McCartney National Bank, thereby leaving a credit balance in favor of said The McCartney National Bank of Nine Thousand Five Hundred Twenty-seven and 39/100 ($9,527.39) Dollars.

Plaintiff further avers that by reason thereof defendant became liable to pay to plaintiff as Receiver aforesaid, said sum of money, namely Nine Thousand Five Hundred Twenty-seven and 39/100 ($9,527.39) Dollars, so deposited by or for the account of The McCartney National Bank with defendant and held by said defendant as a credit to said bank as aforesaid, and being so liable the defendant in consideration thereof then and there promised to pay plaintiff, as Receiver aforesaid, the said sum of money, but although often requested the defendant has refused and still refuses to pay the same, or any part thereof, or the interest thereon as is allowed by law.

Second Count.

Plaintiff avers that the matter in controversy exceeds, exclusive of interest and costs, the sum and value of Three Thousand ($3,000.) Dollars, and is between citizens of different states; that the defendant now is and at all times complained of was a corporation organized under the banking laws of the State of Illinois and conducting a general banking business in Chicago, Illinois that The McCartney National Bank now it and at all times complained of was a corporation organized under the banking laws of the United States of America and prior to the closing of said Bank as hereinafter set forth, conducted a general banking business in Green Bay, Wisconsin.

Plaintiff further acers that this suit is one arising under Section 41 (16) of Title 28 of the United States Code.

Plaintiff further avers that on the evening of May 27, 1931 the Directors of The McCartney National Bank adopted a resolution closing said Bank, and that said The McCartney National Bank failed to open for business on the morning of May 28, 1931; that on said 28th day of May, 1931 the affairs of said Bank were surrendered to and taken charge by the Comptroller of the Currency through his representative, Harry W. Walker, a National Bank Examiner; that on the 29th day of May, 1931 plaintiff was duly appointed as Receiver of The McCartney National Bank by the Comptroller of the Currency; that he duly qualified as such Receiver and that since said 29th day of May, 1931 plaintiff has been and now is the acting Receiver of said The McCartney National Bank, and since said date has had possession of all the books, records and assets of every description of said The McCartney National Bank.

Plaintiff further avers for that whereas, the defendant on the 18th day of November, 1931 in the District aforesaid was indebted to the plaintiff as Receiver aforesaid in the sum of Twelve Thousand ($12,000.) Dollars for goods, chattels and effects before that time sold and delivered by The McCartney National Bank to the defendant at its request; and in the like sum for goods, chattels and effects before that time bargained and sold by The McCartney National Bank to the defendant at its request; and in the like sum for work and services before that time done and bestowed, and materials for the same work furnished by The McCartney National Bank for the defendant at its request; and in the like sum for money before that time lent by The McCartney National Bank to the defendant at its request; and in the like sum for money before that time paid and expended by The McCartney National Bank for the use of the defendant at its request; and in the like sum for money before that time received by the defendant for the use of The McCartney National Bank; and in the like sum for interest on divers sums of money before that time forborne by The McCartney National Bank to the defendant at its request, for divers spaces of time before then elapsed; and in the like sum for money found to be due from the defendant to The McCartney National Bank on an account then and there stated between them; and being so indebted, the defendant in consideration thereof then and there promised to pay the plaintiff as Receiver aforesaid on request the several sums of money so due to him as such Receiver. Yet the defendant, though requested, has not paid the same, or either of them, or any part thereof, but refuses so to do.

9   To the damage of the plaintiff as Receiver aforesaid of Twelve Thousand ($12,000.) Dollars, and therefore he brings his suit.

MILLER, GORHAM & WALES,
Attorneys for Plaintiff.

State of Wisconsin,   } ss.
County of Brown.   }

L. J. BOSWORTH, being first duly sworn, on oath deposes and says that he is the duly appointed, qualified and acting Receiver of The McCartney National Bank, of Green Bay, Wisconsin, and plaintiff in the above entitled suit; that said suit is for the recovery of moneys due from the defendant to the plaintiff as Receiver of The McCartney National Bank, and that there is now due and owing from defendant to plaintiff as Receiver aforesaid, after allowing to said defendant all just credits and set offs, the sum of Nine Thousand Five

Hundred Twenty-seven and 39/100 ($9,527.39) Dollars, together with interest thereon as allowed by law.

L. J. Bosworth,

Subscribed and Sworn to before me this 23 day of November, A. D. 1931.

B. C. Olejniczak,

(Seal)   *Notary Public.*

10   STATEMENT OF ACCOUNT SUED UPON.

Continental Illinois Bank and Trust Company

To

L. J. Bosworth, Receiver of The McCartney National Bank,
Dr.

For goods, chattels and effects sold and delivered by The McCartney National Bank to the defendant	$12,000.00
For goods, chattels and effects bargained and sold by The McCartney National Bank to the defendant	12,000.00
For work and services done and bestowed, and materials for the same work furnished by The McCartney National Bank for the defendant	12,000.00
For money lent by The McCartney National Bank to the defendant	12,000.00
For money paid and expended by The McCartney National Bank for the use of the defendant	12,000.00
For money received by the defendant for the use of The McCartny National Bank	12,000.00
For interest on divers sums of money forborne by The McCartney National Bank to the defendant, for divers spaces of time before then elapsed	12,000.00
For money found to be due from the defendant to The McCartney National Bank on an account then and there stated between them	12,000.00

11   Be it remembered that on this day, to wit, the 24th day of November, 1932, came the plaintiff in said entitled suit, by his attorneys, and filed in the Clerk's office of said Court, a Praecipe praying for the issuance of a Writ of Summons against the defendant, which said Praecipe is in words and figures following, to wit:

12   * * (Caption) * *

The clerk of said court will issue a summons in said cause to said defendants, in a plea of Trespass on the case on Promises to the damage of said plaintiff in the sum of Twelve Thousand Dollars, direct the same to the United States Marshal for said District to execute and make it returnable to the December Term of said Court, 1931.

Dated this 24th day of November, A. D. 1931.

MILLER GORHAM & WALES
Plaintiff's Attorneys.

to

CHARLES M. BATES,
Clerk.

13   On the same day, to wit, the 27th day of November, 1931, a Writ of Summons issued out of the Clerk's office of said Court against said defendant in said above-entitled cause, as prayed for in said Praecipe, which said writ with the return of the Marshal thereon indorsed is in the words and figures following, to wit:

Filed December 14, 1931.

14   * * (Caption) * *

The President of the United States of America to the Marshal of the Northern District of Illinois—Greeting:

We Command You to Summon Continental Illinois Bank and Trust Company, of Chicago, Illinois if found in your District, to be and appear before our Judge of the District Court of the United States for the Northern District of Illinois, on the first day of the next Term thereof, to be holden at Chicago, in the District aforesaid, on the first Third Monday of December next, to answer unto L. J. Bosworth, Receiver of the McCartney National Bank of Green Bay, Wisconsin of a plea of trespass on the case upon promises, to his damages, as he allege, of Twelve Thousand Dollars ($12,000.00), and have you then and there this Writ.

Witness, the Hon Charles E. Woodward, Judge of the District Court of the United States of America, at Chicago aforesaid, this 27th day of November, in the year of our Lord one thousand nine hundred and 31 and of our Independence the 156th year.

CHARLES M. BATES
Clerk.

(Seal)

Served this writ on the within named Continental Illinois Bank and Trust Company of Chicago, Illinois, Assistant Cashier a corporation, by delivering a copy thereof to A. C. Johnson, an agent of said corporation this 11 day of Dec. 1931.

The president of said corporation not found in my District. H. C. W. Laubenheimer, U. S. Marshal By R. D. Holcomb Deputy.

Marshal's Fees

1 service	$2.00
1 miles	.06
Total	$2.06

Dec. 14, I.

15 And on, to wit, the 14th day of December 1931 came the Defendant by its attorneys and filed in the Clerk's office of said Court a certain Appearance in words and figures following, to wit:

16 * * (Caption) * *

We hereby enter the appearance of Continental Illinois Bank and Trust Company, a corporation, defendant herein, and that of ourselves as its attorneys in the above entitled cause.

MAYER, MEYER, AUSTRIAN & PLATT
Attorneys for Defendant.

Dec. 30,

17 And on, to wit, the 30th day of December 1931 came the Defendant by its attorneys and filed in the Clerk's office of said Court a certain Plea and Affidavit of Merits in words and figures following, to wit:

18 * * (Caption) * *

PLEA.

And the defendant, Continental Illinois Bank and Trust Company, by Mayer, Austrian & Platt, its attorneys, comes and defends the wrong and injury when, etc., and says that it did not undertake or promise in manner and form as the plaintiff has above thereof in each court of the declaration complained against it, the defendant, and of this the defendant puts itself upon the country, etc.

MAYER, MEYER, AUSTRIAN & PLATT,
Attorneys for Defendant.

19   * * (Caption) * *

AFFIDAVIT OF MERITS.

State of Illinois } ss.
County of Cook   }

R. G. DANIELSON, being first duyl sworn, on oath deposes and says that he is the cashier and the duly authorized agent in this behalf of the defendant in the above entitled cause; that he verily believes that defendant has a good defense upon the merits to the whole of plaintiff's demand, and that the nature of the defense of the defendant is as follows:

That said The McCartney National Bank, of Green Bay, Wisconsin, was at the time or times referred to in plaintiff's declaration and still is indebted to defendant in a sum in excess of the amount claimed by plaintiff.

That said The McCartney National Bank did not bargain, sell or deliver to plaintiff any goods, chattels or effects;
20 nor has it performed, done or bestowed any work or services to or for plaintiff, nor has it furnished any materials to the defendant; and that said The McCartney National Bank has not loaned any money to defendant nor paid nor expended any money for the use of the defendant; nor has defendant received any money for the use of said The McCartney National Bank; that said The McCartney National Bank has not forborne any sums of money to the defendant for any space of time; that there has been no money found to be due from defendant to said The McCartney National Bank on any accounting had between them, nor has defendant promised to pay plaintiff, as Receiver, any sum of money.

That defendant is not indebted to plaintiff in the sum of Nine Thousand Five Hundred Twenty-seven Dollars and Thirty-nine Cents ($9,527.39), or in any other sum whatsoever.

R. G. DANIELSON

Subscribed And Sworn To before me this 23rd day of December, 1931.

W. A. HERBSTER
Notary Public.

(Seal)

21   And on, to wit, the 7th day of June, 1932, came the
        parties by their attorneys and filed in the Clerk's office
of said Court a certain Stipulation in words and figures following, to wit:

22   * * (Caption) * *

STIPULATION.

Come now the parties to the above entitled cause, by their
respective attorneys, and stipulate that said cause shall be
submitted to the court for hearing without the intervention of
a jury.
        Dated, June 7, 1932.

                    MILLER, GORHAM, WALES & ALAMS
                            Attorneys for Plaintiff
                    MAYER, MEYER, AUSTRIAN & PLATT
                            Attorneys for Defendant.

23   And on, to wit, the 7th day of June, 1932 came the
        Parties by their attorneys and filed in the Clerk's office
of said Court a certain Stipulation in words and figures fol-
        lowing, to wit:

24-30 (Omitted per Stipulation filed Dec. 1, 1932, said stipu-
        lation appearing at page 22, Printed Record.)

31   And on, to wit, the 7th day of June, 1932, came the
        Parties by their attorneys and filed in the Clerk's office
of said Court a certain Amendment to Stipulation in words
        and figures following, to wit:

32-33 (Omitted per stipulation filed Dec. 1, 1932, said
        Amendment to Stipulation appearing at p. 27, Printed
Record.)

34   DEFENDANT'S EXHIBIT 1.

                    Filed June 7, 1932.

    (Omitted per stipulation filed Dec. 1, 1932, said exhibit
appearing at p. 29, Printed Record.)

35   And on, to wit, the 8th day of August, 1932 came the ^{Filed A} ^{1932.}
Plaintiff by his attorneys and filed in the Clerk's office
of said Court a certain Motion in words and figures following, to wit:

36   * * (Caption) * *

MOTION.

Now comes the plaintiff in the above entitled cause and
moves the Court to find the issues in said cause in favor of
the plaintiff and to enter judgment accordingly.

MILLER, GORHAM, WALES & ADAMS
Attorneys for Plaintiff

37   And on, to wit, the 8th day of August, 1932 came the
Defendant by its attorneys and filed in the Clerk's office
of said Court a certain Request for Findings in words and
figures following, to wit:

38   * * (Caption) * *

REQUEST OF THE DEFENDANT, CONTINENTAL IL-
LINOIS BANK AND TRUST COMPANY FOR FIND-
INGS.

Now comes Continental Illinois Bank and Trust Company,
the defendant in the above entitled cause, and hereby requests the court to make the following findings:
   1.   The plaintiff is not entitled to recover any amount
whatsoever herein.
   2.   The defendant is entitled to a judgment in its favor
herein.
   3.   That judgment herein should be entered in favor of
the defendant herein.
   4.   The defendant herein is entitled to off set against the
plaintiff's demand herein an amount equal to plaintiff's demand herein.
   5.   The defendant is entitled to offset herein against plaintiff's claim herein the amount of the draft dated May 27, 1931,
drawn by the McCartney National Bank on Federal Reserve

Bank of Chicago payable to the order of the defendant, Continental Illinois Bank and Trust Company in the sum of
39 $10,823.14 and more specifically described in paragraph
6 of the original stipulation of facts herein.
    Dated June 7, 1932.

                    MAYER, MEYER, AUSTRIAN & PLATT
                    Attorneys for defendant, Continental
                    Illinois Bank and Trust Company

Aug. 6,   40   And on, to-wit, the 6th day of August, 1932 came the
                Plaintiff by his attorneys and filed in the Clerk's office
of said Court a certain Motion in words and figures following, to wit:

41   * * (Caption) * *

                        MOTION.

    Now comes the plaintiff in the above entitled cause and
moves the Court to find as follows:
    1.   The defendant was not the owner of the items which
it forwarded to the McCartney National Bank May 26, 1931,
nor of any credit arising by the receipt and acceptance of
said items by the McCartney National Bank.
    2.   The defendant was not the beneficial owner of the items
which it forwarded to the McCartney National Bank May 26,
1931, nor of any credit arising by the receipt and acceptance
of said items by the McCartney National Bank.
    3.   The defendant was not the owner of the draft issued
by the McCartney National Bank May 27, 1931, and received
    by the defendant May 28, 1931.
42   4.   The defendant was not the beneficial owner of the
        draft issued by the McCartney National Bank May 27,
1931, and received by the defendant May 28, 1931.

                    MILLER GORHAM WALES AND ADAMS
                                Attorneys for Plaintiff

43   And afterwards, to wit, on the 6th day of August, 1932, Entered
1932.
being one of the days of the regular July term of said
Court, in the record of proceedings thereof, in said entitled
cause, before the Honorable Walter C. Lindley, District
Judge, appears the following entry, to wit:

44   *   *   (Caption)   *   *

Saturday, August 6, 1932.

Present: Honorable Walter C. Lindley, Judge of said Court.

This day comes the plaintiff by his attorneys and enters
herein his motion for a finding which motion is overruled as
to the motion and as to each tendered finding to which ruling
of the court the plaintiff by his attorney here and now duly
excepts.

45   And afterwards, to wit, on the 6th day of August, 1932, Filed A
1932.
being one of the days of the regular July term of said
Court, in the record of proceedings thereof, in said entitled
cause, before the Honorable Walter C. Lindley District
Judge, appears the following entry, to wit:

46   *   *   (Caption)   *   *

FINDINGS OF FACT.

1. The Court finds each and every fact set forth in stipulation and amendment to stipulation filed herein as Plaintiff's
and Defendant's Exhibits 1 and 2.

2. The Court finds that each, every and all of said checks
drawn on the McCartney National Bank which were forwarded by the defendant Bank to the McCartney National
Bank on May 26, 1931, for collection and returns in Chicago
exchange, were endorsed: "Pay to the order of Continental-
Illinois Bank and Trust Company" or "Pay to the order of
any bank, banker or trust company."

3. The Court finds that the defendant on May 28, 1931,
which was after it learned that the McCartney National Bank
was closed, made a debit memorandum debiting the account
of the McCartney National Bank with the total amount of the

items which were forwarded by the defendant to the McCartney National Bank on May 26, 1931.

WALTER C. LINDLEY
Judge

August 6, 1932.

Plaintiff allowed an exception as to each of the findings two and three above.

Aug. 6, 47   And afterwards, to wit, on the 6th day of August 1932, being one of the days of the regular July term of said Court, in the record of proceedings thereof, in said entitled cause, before the Honorable Walter C. Lindley District Judge, appears the following entry, to wit:

48   * * (Caption) * *

MEMORANDUM OF THE COURT.

LINDLEY, *District Judge:*

Plaintiff, as receiver for the McCartney National Bank of Green Bay, Wisconsin, brings this suit at law to recover from defendant, Continental Illinois Bank and Trust Company, the sum of $5890.79 on deposit with the latter to the credit of the McCartney Bank and interest thereon. Defendant justifies its refusal to surrender such deposit upon the ground that it rightfully set off against the same a draft issued by the McCartney Bank to defendant in payment of certain customers' checks drawn on the McCartney Bank received by defendant for collection.

The facts are not in dispute. On May 26, 1931 defendant in Chicago forwarded to the McCartney Bank in Green Bay, Wisconsin, one hundred twenty-two checks drawn on the latter, by its depositors, received by the Continental from its customers in the usual course of business, for which credit had been advanced upon the deposit accounts of the customers. On the following day the McCartney Bank, received these checks, charged them against the accounts of the respective drawers thereof, and forwarded to defendant, as remittance therefor, a draft upon the Federal Reserve

49 Bank of Chicago, payable to defendant, for the sum now in controversy, plus certain amounts with which we are not concerned.

Defendant received the draft on May 28, and at 10:30 A. M. presented it to the drawee, who refused to honor it, for the reason, that on May 27th at 9:15 P. M. the directors of the McCartney Bank had adopted a resolution closing same. On May 28th prior to the presentation of the dratf aforesaid to the drawee, te comptroller of the currency took possession of the Wisconsin Bank, and on May 29th plaintiff was appointed receiver and qualified as such. The Federal Reserve Bank, prior to the presentation of the draft as aforesaid, on the morning of May 28th had received a telegram from the comptroller, notifying it of the happenings aforesaid, and directing it to honor no outstanding drafts of the McCartney Bank. The Continental was notified of the existing status at 11:15 A. M. of May 28th.

Each of the checks mentioned was received by defendant under an express agreement with its depositor, that in handling same it acted as "collecting agent" charged with no duty other than to exercise due care and granted a lien upon all proceeds for charges and expenses. None of the defendant depositors withdrew any of the deposit credits represented by said checks before defendant received advice of the closing of the McCartney Bank. On May 29th defendant charged back to the account of its customers the respective amounts of said checks and notified the customers of such action.

The sole question involved is as to the right of defendant to set off as against the deposit account of the McCartney Bank existing on May 28th, the amount of the dishonored draft drawn by the former.

The parties agree that the rights of the parties are fixed as of the date of the closing of the McCartney Bank. If there were ever any doubt that the rights of interested parties are to be determined by the status existing at the time of insolvency. It has been complete dissolved by such decisions as *Scott* v. *Armstrong* 146 U. S. 499.

The McCartney Bank, by vote of its directors, closed at 9 P. M. May 27th. At that time, the Continental owed to it the deposit here in controversy, and at that time it owed to the Continental, as collecting agent for the latter's customers, the amount of the draft. Indeed, upon May 26th it owed the Continental in the same capacity the amount of the checks forwarded by the latter to it for collection; the giving of the draft was but the written acknowledgment of such debt. Obviously, then, before the bank closed, in the usual course of business, the mutual credits and debits had arisen. Nothing transpiring thereafter could alter the legal rights of the parties. Each could set off against its debt due the other, the credit due it from the other. The clothier having a debt against his butcher, may not complain if the latter sets off against the debt the clothier's bill for beef-steak purchased the night before the clother became insolvent—(*Scott v. Armstrong, supra*).

If the McCartney Bank and defendant had by collusion, upon the eve of insolvency, with notice of same by defendant, so arranged matters as to create a new basis for set-off of mutual debts and credits, a different situation would exist. But, here the facts were fixed in the usual course of business; there was no bad faith working to the disadvantage of other creditors, out of the usual course of business to deplete the estate—Consequently there was no preference of the Continental within the inhibition of the Acts of Congress governing National Banks. In discussing the effect of a similar statute, the Supreme Court in *Scott v. Armstrong supra*, said:

"The argument is that these sections by implication forbide this set-off because they require that after the redemption of the circulating notes has been fully provided for, the assets shall be ratably distributed among the creditors, and that no preferences given or suffered, in contemplation of or after committing the act of insolvency. * * * * * We do not regard this position as

51   tenable. Undoubtedly, any disposition by a national bank, being insolvent or in contemplation of insolvency, of its choses in action, securities, or other assets, made to prevent their application to the payment of its circulating notes, or to prefer one creditor to another, is forbidden; but liens, equities, or rights arising by express agreement, or, implied from the nature of the dealings between the parties, or by operation of law, prior to insolvency and not in contemplation thereof, are not invalidated. The provisions of the Act are not directed against all liens, securities, pledges, or equities, whereby one creditor may obtain a greater payment than another, but against those given or arising after or in contemplation of insolvency. Where a set-off is otherwise valid, it is not perceived how its allowance can be considered a preference, and it is clear that it is only the balance, if any, after the set-off is deducted which can justly be held to form part of the assets of the insolvent."

The Court pointed out a clear distinction between the facts therein involved and those where the attempted set-off arises from acts done after insolvency, saying:

"The state of case where the claim sought to be offset is acquired after the act of insolvency is far otherwise, for the rights of the parties become fixed as of that time, and to sustain such a transfer would defeat the object of these provisions."

Other Courts have had before them situations in every way comparable to that now before the Court and following the same reasoning, reached conclusions consistent only with that of the case cited. In *Keys, Receiver, etc.* v. *Federal Reserve Bank*, (unreported) Judge Morris, commenting upon similar facts said:

52   "It is not apparent that upon the clearance being had between the Clarkfield banks defendant had the right to a credit with the First National Bank of Clarkfield for this amount and to charge the same to the account of said bank. That credit was given, but the charge was not made. It seems to me that defendant then had a right of action against that bank for said amount in its own name and in its own right. And if this is true, it is clear it has had that right ever since, and therefore has the right of set off. The Receiver, the plaintiff here, took the assets of the bank as a mere trustee for creditors, and not for value and without notice, and, in the absence of statute to the contrary, subject to all claims and defenses that might have been interposed as against the insolvent bank. The subsequent charging back of the checks by defendant or the subsequent statements of counsel for the defendant in his letters would not in any way affect the conclusion. The recovery of the set off here will fully protect the plaintiff and he has no interest in, and is not concerned to inquire into, what was done between defendant and the banks depositing these checks or what advice has been given to defendant by its counsel, *Elmquist* v. *Markot*, 45 Minn. 305, *Vanstrum* v. *Liljengren*, 37 Minn. 191."

"It seems to me that the rights of the parties became fixed as of the time of the closing of the bank. *Scott* v. *Armstrong*, 146 U. S. 499-511. At that time defendant had a right of action against plaintiff's insolvent for the amount of the checks, whether or not they were only received by it as an agent for collection and conditional credit, and whether or not the endorsements thereon were restricted or unrestricted. General Statutes of Minnesota 1913, Section 5848 and 5849. The subsequent ownership of the checks is unimportant. There was no

defense as to the checks and no defense as to the credit
arising therefrom on the books of the insolvent bank.
The plaintiff has no standing to inquire into the relations between defendant and its depositing bank.
Neither the insolvent nor its receiver has any concern
with the question of the ownership of the checks, unless
a defense be shown as against the endorsers or drawers
thereof, or that defendant became the holder thereof
after the closing of the bank for insolvency, or after
knowledge of its insolvency. There is no such showing,
and on the contrary the opposite appears. *Farmers Deposit National Bank* v. *Penn. Bank*, 123 Pa. 283, *Penn.
Bank* v. *Farmers Deposit National Bank*, 130 Pa. 209.''

53   See also *Storing* v. *First Natl. Bank*, 28 Fed. (2) 587
(C. C. A. 8), *Farmers Bank* v. *Penn. Bank*, 123 Pa. St.
283; 16 Atl. 761; *Midland Natl. Bank* v. *First State Bank*,
222 N. W. 274. From an examination of cases cited in this
connection, I believe all of them capable of reconciliation
with those here relied upon and to differ in conclusions
therefrom only because of facts occurring after insolvency,
or because of collusion, resulting in illegal preferences.

But it is earnestly urged that the set-off is not mutual;
that the deposit is owed by the Continental in its personal
capacity and the draft held by it in a fiduciary capacity as
agent for its customers, and that the two cannot be set-off
against each other.

The law will not allow set-offs between parties not mutually liable. A may not set off B's debt to him against C's
claim against A. Going a step further, A may not set off
A's claim as trustee against B's claim against him personally. There is as much difference between A and B as between A and A as trustee. So agents, trustees, executors
and similar fiduciaries may not ordinarily pay their individual debts by cancelling fiduciary demands held for others—
Libby v. *Hopkins*, 104 U. S. 303; *Hanover Natl. Bank* v.
Suddoth, 215 U. S. 122.

The checks here involved were indorsed ''Pay to the order
of the Continental-Ill. Bank & Trust Company'' or ''Pay to
any bank or bankers.'' Such indorsements rested title in
the Continental. Whether considered as general or restricted in character, they sufficiently passed title—thus Section 37 of the Uniform Negotiable Instruments Act is as follows:

''A restrictive indorsement confers upon the indorser

the right (1) to receive payment of the instrument; (2) to bring any action thereon that the indorser could bring."

Defendant, therefore, might have sued upon the checks in its personal capacity. It follows that it may, therefore, set same off at law. Thus in *Keys etc.* v. *Federal Reserve Bank, supra.,* Judge Morris said:

54   "Immediately upon the failure of the Sioux Falls bank to pay, the plaintiff had a cause of action against it for the amount which it had collected and did not pay. It had the legal title, so to speak, to the dishonored drafts drawn by the Sioux Falls bank. Whatever right it had arose upon the failure of the bank to remit what it received, and its right was protected by the security of the pledge agreement. There is no reason why the Sioux Falls bank or its creditors should have the $19,000 which came from its collections for the plaintiff when the pledge agreement secured its payment to the plaintiff, and the plaintiff be compelled to seek a remedy by participating in the insolvent estate of the bank. It was right that the collateral held under the pledge agreement should respond to the payment of the moneys collected. The charging off of the credits was a matter between the plaintiff bank and its customers. Neither the South Dakota bank nor its creditors nor those representing them in this action should gain by it."

An interesting case is *Farmers etc. Bank* v. *Penn. Bank, supra.,* where the Court reversed the trial C, saying:

    "In a suit brought by the assignee of the Penn Bank against the said Farmers Deposit Bank to recover a balance of $23,218.59, admittedly due the Penn Bank at the time of its failure, the Farmers Deposit Bank attempted to use the check of $88,000 as a set-off. The court below instructed the jury that the latter bank could not so use it. This is the one error of the case and it runs all through it.

    The theory of this ruling was that the check belonged to the Germania Savings Bank, and a large amount of time was wasted in trying this unimportant fact. Of what possible concern was it to the Penn Bank whether the defendant held it for collection or for value. It had no defence to the check in the hands of either bank. If there had been a defence as to the Germania then the Penn Bank might have called upon the defendant to show that it had paid value. But as the case stood—with no defence as to either bank—it had no standing to inquire into the relations between the defendant and the Germania, any more than if the check had been presented at its counter and payment demanded before its insolvency.

If we concede that the defendant was a mere collecting bank, so far as this check was concerned, it does not alter the case. As such its title was sufficient to maintain a suit in its own name. This is settled law: *Brown v. Clark*, 14 Pa. 469; *Ward v. Tyler*, 52 Pa. 393. It if could maintain a suit on this check in its own name, it is difficult to see any good reason why it could not set the check off in a suit against it by the assignee of the Penn Bank. The rights of the assignee rise no higher than those of his assignor. Neither the Penn Bank nor its assignee has any concern with the question of the ownership of the check, unless a defence be shown as against the Germania, or that the defendant became the holder after the assignment. As no defense was set up against 55   the check in the hands of any one, and as it is an undisputed fact that the defendant became the lawful holder thereof several days before the assignment, we are all of opinion that the set-off should have been allowed.''

No good reason occurs to me why one who may sue upon a draft or upon check in his own name may not set same off as against a debt.

The situation is not to be confused with cases where banks were charged with notice of third persons' interest on deposits in the name of the debtor, and therefore forbidden to use such deposits as set-offs against the nominal depositor. Such was the situation in *U. S.* v. *Butterworth-Judson Corporation*, 267 U. S. 387; *Central Natl. Bank* v. *Conn, Mutual Co.*, 104 U. S. 54 and other cases cited by plaintiff.

In view of the foregoing there will be a finding of the issues in behalf of the defendant accordingly, and judgment in favor of defendant and against plaintiff, dismissing the suit, in bar of action, and for costs.

WALTER C. LINDLEY,
United States District Judge.

Dated August 6th, 1932.

56 And afterwards, to wit, on the 6th day of August, ^{Enter} 1932, being one of the days of the regular July term of said Court, in the record of proceedings thereof, in said entitled cause, before the Honorable Walter C. Lindley, District Judge, appears the following entry, to wit:

57   * * (Caption) * *

Saturday, August 6, 1932.

Present: Honorable Walter C. Lindley, Judge of said Court.

The Court having heretofore heard the evidence by the parties adduced and being now fully advised in the premises finds the issues for the defendant, therefore it is considered by the Court that the plaintiff take nothing by his aforesaid action that the defedant go hence without day to have and recover of and from the plaintiff its costs and charges in this behalf expended to be paid in due course of administration.

64   * * (Caption) * *   Bill o tion

BILL OF EXCEPTIONS.

Be It Remembered that heretofore, on to-wit, Thursday, June 7, 1932, the same being one of the judicial days of said term of said Court, the above entitled cause came on to be heard upon the issues joined herein, before his Honor Walter C. Lindley, sitting as a Judge of said Court without a jury, a jury having been duly waived by the parties, by a written stipulation in words and figures as follows, to-wit: (Title of Court and cause omitted.)

Stipulation.

Come now the parties to the above entitled cause by their respective attorneys, and stipulate that said cause shall be submitted to the Court for hearing without the intervention of a jury.

Dated, June 7, 1932.

(Signed MILLER, GORHAM, WALES & ADAMS
Attorneys for Plaintiff
(Signed MAYER, MEYER, AUSTRIAN & PLATT
Attorneys for Defendant.

65   Whereupon, the parties respectively offered and. introduced the following evidence and exhibits of evidence, and the following evidence was rejected, and objections and motions were made and rulings of the court were entered and exceptions taken by the parties, all as follows, to-wit:

Appearances:

> Messrs. Miller, Gorham, Wales & Adams, By Mr. Amos C. Miller, Mr. Henry W. Wales, representing the plaintiff;

> Messrs. Mayer, Meyer, Austrian & Platt, By Mr. Frank D. Mayer, representing the defendant.

And thereupon the plaintiff, by Mr. Miller, his attorney, offered in evidence a stipulation of facts entitled "Stipulation," and a further stipulation entitled "Amendment to the Stipulation;" which said documents were marked as PLAINTIFF'S and DEFENDANT'S EXHIBIT 1 and 2, and offered and received in evidence and read to the Court in the following words and figures, to-wit:

66   PLAINTIFF'S EXHIBIT 1.

* * (Caption) * *

STIPULATION.

Come now the parties to the above entitled cause, by their respective attorneys, and stipulate that said cause shall be submitted to the Court for hearing without the intervention of a jury, and further stipulate that said Court shall find the facts as follows:

1. That this is a suit for winding up the affairs of a National Bank and is brought by the Receiver of The McCartney National Bank to recover from the defendant, Continental Illinois Bank and Trust Company, the sum of Nine Thousand Five Hundred Twenty-seven and 39/100 ($9,527.39) Dollars.

2. That the defendant now is, and at all times complained of was a corporation organized under the banking laws of the State of Illinois conducting a general banking business in Chicago, Illinois.

67   3.   That The McCartney National Bank is, and at all times complained of was a corporation organized under the banking laws of the United States of America conducting a general banking business in Green Bay, Wisconsin.

4.   That on the evening of May 27, 1931 at 9:15 o'clock the Directors of The McCartney National Bank adopted a resolution closing said bank; that said The McCartney National Bank failed to open for business on the morning of May 28, 1931, and that on said 28th day of May, 1931, the affairs of said bank were surrendered to and taken in charge by the Comptroller of the Currency through his representative, Harry W. Walker, a National Bank Examiner; that on the 29th day of May, 1931, the plaintiff, L. J. Bosworth, was duly appointed as Receiver of The McCartney National Bank and duly qualified as such Receiver, and that since said date has been and now is the acting receiver of said bank; that under the direction of the Comptroller of the Currency plaintiff took possession of all the books, records and assets of every description of said bank on said 29th day of May, 1931.

5.   That on the 26th day of May, 1931, the defendant bank, Continental Illinois Bank and Trust Company, forwarded to The McCartney National Bank for collection and returns in Chicago Exchange one hundred twenty-two (122) checks drawn on said The McCartney National Bank which defendant had received from a number of its depositors, and 68   for which said checks credit had been given to said respective depositors by Continental Illinois Bank and Trust Company and which said checks aggregated the sum of Ten Thousand Eight Hundred Twenty-three and 14/100 ($10,823.14) Dollars; that each of said checks was drawn upon The McCartney National Bank by a depositor of that bank.

6.   That on the 27th day of May, 1931, The McCartney National Bank received said checks from the defendant and charged the same to the respective accounts of its customers who had issued said checks, and that on said 27th day of May, 1931 said The McCartney National Bank in remittance for said checks issued its draft for the sum of Ten Thousand Eight Hundred Twenty-three and 14/100 ($10,823.14) Dollars on Federal Reserve Bank of Chicago, payable to the order of defendant bank, and that said draft was received by defendant in the early morning mail on May 28, 1931.

7.   That said draft for Ten Thousand Eight Hundred Twenty-three and 14/100 ($10,823.14) Dollars so drawn by The McCartney National Bank to defendant was presented

by defendant to Federal Reserve Bank of Chicago, Illinois, before 10:30 A. M. on the said 28th day of May, 1931, and payment thereof was refused by said Federal Reserve Bank of Chicago; that on said 28th day of May, 1931, and prior to the presentation of said draft by defendant to Federal Reserve Bank of Chicago, the Comptroller of the Currency through Harry W. Walker, National Bank Examiner as aforesaid,

69   had taken charge of the affairs of the said The McCartney National Bank, and that on said 28th day of May, 1931, and prior to the presentation of said draft to Federal Reserve Bank of Chicago, said Federal Reserve Bank of Chicago had received notification by telegram from the Comptroller of the Currency and from said Harry W. Walker, National Bank Examiner in charge of The McCartney National Bank as aforesaid, that said bank had closed and to stop payment on all outstanding drafts of said The McCartney National Bank; that at 11:15 o'clock in the forenoon of said 28th day of May, 1931, the defendant received notification by telegram from Harry W. Walker, National Bank Examiner in charge of said The McCartney National Bank, that said The McCartney National Bank had suspended.

8. That for some time prior to May 28, 1931 (the date of the closing of The McCartney National Bank) The McCartney National Bank had and maintained with defendant bank, Continental Illinois Bank and Trust Company, a deposit account; that at the opening of business on May 28, 1931 and before said defendant bank had any notice of the closing of The McCartney National Bank, there was a balance to the credit of The McCartney National Bank of Six Thousand Three and 41/100 ($6,003.41) Dollars; that subsequently, on said May 28, 1931 and before the defendant bank had any notice of the closing of The McCartney National Bank, deposits aggregating Five Thousand Three Hundred Ninety-eight and 14/100 ($5,398.14) Dollars and withdrawals aggregating Four Hundred Four and 70/100 ($404.70) Dollars were made, which left a credit balance in favor of The

70   McCartney National Bank at the time that the defendant bank received notice of the closing of The McCartney National Bank of Ten Thousand Nine Hundred Ninety-seven and 12/100 ($10,997.12) Dollars.

9. That subsequent to May 28, 1931 items for which The McCartney National Bank had received credit from the defendant bank were returned to the Continental Illinois Bank and Trust Company unpaid (which items were returned to

The McCartney National Bank), reducing said balance to Ten Thousand Forty-two and 39/100 ($10,042.39) Dollars; that there was included in the credit of Ten Thousand Forty-two and 39/100 ($10.042.39) Dollars the sum of Five Hundred Fifteen ($515.) Dollars, representing a bond and coupon collection, which amount was subsequently paid over to plaintiff as Receiver of The McCartney National Bank, thereby reducing the bank balance of said The McCartney National Bank to Nine Thousand Five Hundred Twenty-seven and 39/100 ($9,527.39) Dollars; that if plaintiff is entitled to recover in this action, judgment should be entered in his favor against defendant for said sum of Nine Thousand Five Hundred Twenty-seven and 39/100 ($9,527.39) Dollars, together with interest thereon if allowable by law.

10. That each, every and all of said checks drawn on The McCartney National Bank which were forwarded by defendant bank to The McCartney National Bank on May 26, 1931 for collection and returns in Chicago Exchange were accepted for deposit by the defendant bank from its customers under the following written agreement between defendant bank and its customers respectively:

71   "In receiving and handling items for deposit or collection (including items received in payment of collections) this Bank acts only as depositor's collecting agent and assumes no responsibility beyond the exercise of due care. All items are credited or cashed subject to final payment in cash or solvent credits. This Bank will not be liable for default or negligence of its correspondents, nor for losses in transit, and no correspondent shall be liable except for its own negligence. It is optional but not obligatory, to request certification in any case. This Bank or its correspondents may, as depositor's agent, send items, directly or indirectly, to any bank or to any drawee, acceptor or payor, and accept draft, check or credit as conditional payment in lieu of cash. It may charge back may item at any time before final payment, whether returned or not, also any item drawn on this Bank not good at close of business on day deposited. It may decline to honor or pay checks drawn against conditional credits. This Bank shall have a lien on all items handled by it and on the proceeds thereof for its charges, expenses (including court costs and attorney's fees) and any advances made by it in connection therewith.

"It may transmit any item for collection to any Federal Reserve Bank and such item shall be subject to the rules and regulations of such Federal Reserve Bank or of the Federal Reserve Board now in force or hereafter promulgated.

"Items payable in the City of Chicago, or in any suburb thereof, may be collected through the Chicago Clearing House Association (in which event they may be carried over for presentation through the Clearing House on the following business day) and will be subject to its rules and regulations now in force or hereafter adopted; or they may be collected in any manner hereinbefore provided or contemplated.

"This Bank endeavors to forward items payable outside of Chicago on day of receipt, but it is understood that they need not be forwarded until the following business day."

11. That prior to the receipt of notice by the defendant bank of the closing of The McCartney National Bank there were no withdrawals by any of the customers of defendant bank against the credits given to them, respectively, by reason of the deposit of said checks drawn upon The McCartney National Bank, nor were there at the time said defendant bank received notice of the closing of The McCartney National Bank any existing overdrafts on the part of any of said customers.

12. That subsequent to the 28th day of May, 1931 and on the 29th day of May, 1931 and following days, defendant bank charged back to the accounts of its customers the amounts of the checks on The McCartney National Bank so deposited by them respectively, and notified its customers of such action.

13. That the checks aggregating Ten Thousand Eight Hundred Twenty-three and 14/100 ($10,823.14) Dollars sent by defendant bank to The McCartney National Bank on May 26, 1931 were never returned to the defendant bank but were cancelled by said The McCartney National Bank and since the closing of said bank have been delivered by the Receiver to the respective makers thereof.

14. It is further hereby stipulated by and between the parties to the above entitled cause, by their respective attorneys, that each of the parties hereto shall have the right to introduce at any time during the hearing of this cause evidence additional to but not contradictory of the facts set forth in this stipulation.

MILLER, GORHAM & WALES
Attorneys for Plaintiff.
MAYER, MEYER, AUSTRIAN & PLATT
Attorneys for Defendant.

73   PLAINTIFF'S EXHIBIT 2.

*   *   (Caption)   *   *

AMENDMENT TO STIPULATION.

Now Come the parties to the above entitled cause, by their respective attorneys, and stipulate that the original Stipulation of Facts entered into between the parties hereto be amended as follows:

1. It is agreed that among the items forwarded by Continental Illinois Bank and Trust Company to The McCartney National Bank on May 26, 1931 for collection and returns, as set forth in Paragraph 5 of the original stipulation herein, were certain checks aggregating $4131.96, which had been forwarded by State Savings Bank of Frankfort, Michigan, to Continental Illinois Bank and Trust Company for collection; that the total amount of said check is 38.17% of the total amount of the checks forwarded on said date by said Continental Illinois Bank and Trust Company to said The McCartney National Bank.

2. It is further stipulated and agreed that the indebtedness based upon said $4131.96 of checks may be withdrawn as an offset by said Continental Illinois Bank and Trust Company and a separate claim may be filed for said sum against The McCartney National Bank by said State Savings
74   Bank of Frankfort, Michigan, without prejudice to the rights of either party hereto.

3. That the balance of the deposit of The McCartney National Bank with the Continental Illinois Bank and Trust Compny, which defendnt seeks to apply as an offset to plaintiff's claim was $9527.39; that defendant is willing to pay to plaintiff 38.17% of said balance of $9527.39, being the sum of $3636.60, if said withdrawal is made and said payment is accepted without prejudice to the rights of the defendant.

4. It is further stipulated and agreed that said Continental Illinois Bank and Trust Company may pay the plaintiff herein the said sum of $3636.60 without prejudice to the rights of either party hereto, and that the amount which plaintiff seeks to recover herein shall be $5890.79, together with interest at the legal rate on the sum of $9527.39 to the date of the payment of said sum of $3636.60 if it shall be adjudicated that plaintiff is entitled to interest, and interest

thereafter at the legal rate on the said sum o $5890.79, if it be adjudicated that plaintiff is entitled to interest.

5. It is further stipulated and agreed that the plaintiff, by a letter dated June 9, 1931, and received by the Continental Illinois Bank and Trust Company, June 10, 1931, requested and demanded that the defendant pay the sum of $9527.39 to the plaintiff as receiver for The McCartney National Bank.

6. It is further stipulated and agreed that, except as expressly amended hereby, the original stipulation of facts between the parties hereto shall remain in full force and effect.

MILLER GORHAM AND WALES
Attorneys for Plaintiff.
MAYER MEYER AUSTRIAN & PLATT
Attorneys for Defendant

75 And thereupon the defendant to maintain the issues on its part introduced and offered the following evidence:

N. B. GROVES called as a witness on behalf of the defendant, having been duly and regularly sworn testified as follows:

Direct Examination by Mr. Mayer.

My name is N. B. Groves and address 6654 Ogola Avenue, Chicago. I have been employed by the Continental-Illinois Bank and Trust Company, the defendant in this suit, for twenty-five years, and I am employed as supervisor of the Transit Department. The items which pass through the Transit Department are cash items that are accepted for immediate credit. That is the type of item we are dealing with in this suit, that was sent to the McCartney National Bank. I have the debit memo, debiting the account of that bank. (The document was marked Defendant's Exhibit 1, for identification) This is the memorandum which was made in our books upon learning that the McCartney National Bank was closed. (Defendant offered the document in evidence, as DEFENDANT'S EXHIBIT 1, but the plaintiff objected to it as immaterial and the Court ruled that it might be received in evidence subject to the objection. Thereupon said document was received in evidence as DEFENDANT'S EXHIBIT 1, and is the following words and figures, to-wit:

DEFENDANT'S EXHIBIT 1.

Continental Illinois Bank and Trust Company
Chicago, Illinois

Date May 28, 1931

Representing our cash letter of May 26, for which actual payment has not been received.

[Stamped. Do not enter on statement or file with checks]
Debit

Bank Suspended Account
McCartney National Bank,
Green Bay, Wisconsin.

Charge Account
$10,823.14

Advised by .... Dept Transit HTZ
Approved N. B. Groves

76   I can state the nature of the endorsements that were on the checks which were forwarded to the McCartney National Bank.

Q. What were those endorsements?

Mr. Miller: I object to that on the ground it is not the best evidence.

Court: Well, he may answer it subject to the objection.

A. Checks would be endorsed: "Pay to the order of Continental Illinois Bank and Trust Company," or "Pay to the order of any bank, banker or trust company."

Cross-Examination by Mr. Miller.

I don't recall just when my recollection was first prompted to the particular subject as to how those checks were endorsed. It was a month ago, or two months ago. I handle a great many items with and among banks of that character every day. All of these transit items have endorsements of that character. Of course they may bear any personal endorsement for items that are cashed over the counter at the paying teller's window; they may have a personal endorsement but all our customers who deposit items are furnished with a stamp that reads in the way I mentioned. I am testifying not from any particular recollection of this matter, but as to the general custom. It is possible that it is a custom that is not always followed.

Whereupon the defendant rested its case.

The foregoing was all the evidence offered, received or heard upon the trial of this cause.

Thereupon the plaintiff moved the Court to find the issues in favor of the plaintiff and to enter judgment accordingly and prestnted a written motion in the following words and figures. (Title of Court and Cause omitted.)

77   MOTION.

Now comes the plaintiff in the above entitled cause and moves the Court to find the issues in said cause in favor of the plaintiff and to enter judgment accordingly.

(Signed) MILLER, GORHAM, WALES & ADAMS
Attorneys for Plaintiff

Whereupon defendant moved the Court to make certain findings and presented a written motion in the following words and figures, to-wit: (Title of Court and Cause omitted.)

REQUEST OF THE DEFENDANT, CONTINENTAL ILLINOIS BANK AND TRUST COMPANY, FOR FINDINGS.

Now comes Continental Illinois Bank and Trust Company, the defendant in the above entitled cause, and hereby requests the court to make the following findings:

1. The plaintiff is not entitled to recover any amount whatsoever herein.

2. The defendant is entitled to a judgment in its favor herein.

3. That judgment herein should be entered in favor of the defendant herein.

4. The defendant herein is entitled to off set against the plaintiff's demand herein an amount equal to plaintiff's demand herein.

5. The defendant is entitled to offset herein against plaintiff's claim herein the amount of the draft dated May 27, 1931, drawn by the McCartney National Bank on Federal Reserve Bank of Chicago payable to the order of the defendant, Continental Illinois Bank and Trust Company in the sum of $10,823.14 and more specifically described in paragraph 6 of the original stipulation of facts herein.

78   Dated June 7, 1932.

MAYER, MEYER, AUSTRIAN & PLATT,
*Attorneys for defendant, Continental Illinois
Bank and Trust Company.*

And thereupon the plaintiff moved the Court to strike the evidence introduced by the defendant, subject to the plaintiff's objection, to the effect that the defendant debited the account of the McCartney National Bank upon learning that it was closed, on the ground that said evidence was immaterial, and to exclude Defendant's Exhibit 1 on the ground that said exhibit was immaterial, and further moved the Court not to consider this evidence or this exhibit in consideration of the case.

The Court denied said motion and ruled that said evidence and said exhibit were admissible, to which action of the Court in overruling his said motion and in admitting said evidence plaintiff, by his attorneys, then and there duly excepted.

Thereupon the plaintiff moved the Court to strike the evidence introduced by the defendant, subject to the plaintiff's objection, relating to the character of the endorsements on the items forwarded to the McCartney National Bank, on the ground that said evidence is not the best evidence and on the further ground that it is immaterial, and to exclude said evidence in consideration of the case.

The Court denied said motion and ruled that said evidence was admissible, to which action of the Court in overruling his said motion and in admitting said evidence the plaintiff, by his attorneys, then and there duly excepted.

Thereupon, after argument of counsel to the Court and the submission of briefs and authorities, the Court took the case under advistment.

Thereafter, on, to-wit, the sixth day of August, 1932, the plaintiff presented to the Court a written motion request-
79 ing special findings of fact, which said written motion was in words and figures as follows, to wit:
(Title of Court and Cause omitted.)

MOTION.

Now comes the plaintiff in the above entitled cause and moves the Court to find as follows:

1. The defendant was not the owner of the items which it forwarded to the McCartney National Bank May 26, 1931, nor of any credit arising by the receipt and acceptance of said items by the McCartney National Bank.

2. The defendant was not the beneficial owner of the items which it forwarded to the McCartney National Bank May 26,

1931, nor of any credit arisng by the receipt and acceptance of said items by the McCartney National Bank.

3. The defendant was not the owner of the draft issued by the McCartney National Bank May 27, 1931, and received by the defendant May 28, 1931.

4. The defendant was not the beneficial owner of the draft issued by the McCartney National Bank May 27, 1931, and received by the defendant May 28, 1931.

(Signed) MILLER, GORHAM, WALES AND ADAMS
Attorneys for Plaintiff

And thereupon, on the sixth day of August, 1932, the Court overruled the foregoing motion of the plaintiff for special findings of fact, and refused to make each and every of said findings of fact, to which action of the Court in overruling said motion and in refusing to make said findings of fact, and each of said findings of fact, the plaintiff, by his attorneys, duly excepted.

80   And thereupon, on said sixth day of August, 1932, the Court made and filed the following findings of fact:
(Title of Court and Cause omitted.)

FINDINGS OF FACT.

1. The Court finds each and every fact set forth in stipulation and amendment to stipulation filed herein as Plaintiff's and Defendant's Exhibits 1 and 2.

2. The Court finds that each, every and all of said checks drawn on the McCartney National Bank which were forwarded by the defendant Bank to the McCartney National Bank on May 26, 1931, for collection and returns in Chicago exchange, were endorsed: "Pay to the order of Continental-Illinois Bank and Trust Company" or "Pay to the order of any bank, banker or trust company."

3. The Court finds that the defendant on May 28, 1931, which was after it learned that the McCartney National Bank was closed, made a debit memorandum debiting the account of the McCartney National Bank with the total amount of the items which were forwarded by the defendant to the McCartney National Bank on May 26, 1931.

(Signed) WALTER C. LINDLEY
Judge

to which findings of fact numbered 2 and 3, and to each of said findings of fact, the plaintiff, by his attorneys, then and there duly excepted.

Thereupon, on the sixth day of August, 1932, the Court overruled plaintiff's motion to find the issues in favor of the plaintiff and to enter judgment accordingly, to which ruling of the Court the plaintiff, by his attorneys, then and there duly excepted.

81   And thereupon, on said sixth day of August, 1932, the Court filed a memorandum of opinion in said cause.

And thereupon, on said sixth day of August, 1932, the Court found the issues against the plaintiff and in favor of the defendant, to which ruling of the Court the plaintiff, by his attorneys, then and there duly excepted.

And thereupon the plaintiff moved the Court to grant a new trial, which motion the Court denied and to which ruling of the Court in so denying said motion for new trial the plaintiff, by his attorneys, then and there duly excepted.

Whereupon the plaintiff, by his attorneys, moved the Court to arrest judgment, but the Court denied said motion, to which ruling of the Court the plaintiff, by his attorneys, then and there duly excepted.

Thereupon, on the sixth day of August, 1932, the Court, over the objection and exception of the plaintiff, entered judgment in favor of the defendant and against the plaintiff, dismissing the suit with costs assessed against the plaintiff, to which action of the Court in entering said judgment the plaintiff, by his attorneys, then and there duly excepted.

And thereafter, on the twenty-sixth day of August, 1932, being one of the days of the July Term of said Court, at which the judgment in this cause was entered, the Court entered an order extending the time within which the plaintiff might have his bill of exceptions signed, allowed and filed to and including the third day of October, 1932.

And at the trial of said cause such proceedings
82   were had, such objections to evidence and such offers of evidence, and such motions and such rulings by the Court were made, such exceptions were taken and saved at the respective times to the several rulings and actions excepted to, as are indicated in the foregoing pages, and which constituted all the proceedings had at the trial of said cause.

Forasmuch as the matters and things above set forth do not fully appear of record, the plaintiff tenders and presents the foregoing as his bill of exceptions in said cause and prays that the same may be settled, allowed and signed and sealed and made a part of the record in said cause by this Court pursuant to the law in such cases.

And said bill of exceptions, containing all of the evidence offered or adduced by any of the parties to this cause, and containing all of the rulings of the Court upon the trial, is accordingly settled, allowed and signed and sealed by the Court on this 30th day of September, A. D. 1932.

WALTER C. LINDLEY   (Seal)
Judge.

It is hereby stipulated by and between the attorneys for the respective parties hereto that the foregoing bill of exceptions contains all the evidence given and proceedings had on the trial of this action, and that it is correct in all respects, and that the same may be approved, allowed, settled and ordered filed and made a part of the record herein by the Honorable Walter C. Lindley, the Judge who presided at the trial of said cause, without further or other notice to defendant or its counsel.

Dated, this 29th day of September, A. D. 1932.

MILLER, GORHAM, WALES AND ADAMS
Attorneys for Plaintiff.
MAYER, MEYER, AUSTRIAN & PLATT
Attorneys for Defendant.

83   (Endorsed) * * (Caption) * * Bill of Exceptions Filed Sep 30 1932 Charles M. Bates, Clerk. Miller, Gorham, Wales and Adams, One La Salle Street, Telephones: Central 5428-5432, Chicago, Illinois, Attorneys for Plaintiff.

Sept. 30,
2.   84   And on, to wit, the 30th day of September, 1932 came the Plaintiff by his attorneys and filed in the Clerk's office of said Court a certain Notice in words and figures following, to wit:

85   * * (Caption) * *

NOTICE.

To: Messrs. Mayer, Meyer, Austrian & Platt Attorneys for Defendant:

Please Take Notice that on Friday, September 30, 1932, at ten o'clock in the forenoon, or as soon thereafter as counsel can be heard, we shall appear before his Honor Judge Walter C. Lindley, in the Federal Building, Chicago, Illinois, and present a petition for appeal, and ask for an order allowing an appeal, without bond, in the above entitled cause, and present a bill of exceptions for approval; at which time and place you may appear if you so see fit.

MILLER, GORHAM, WALES & ADAMS,
Attorneys for Plaintiff.

Received a copy of the foregoing Notice, together with copy of the petition mentioned therein, this 29th day of September, A. D. 1932.

MAYER, MEYER, AUSTRIAN & PLATT

86 And on, to wit, the 30th day of September, 1932 came the Plaintiff by his attorneys and filed in the Clerk's office of said Court a certain Petition for Appeal in words and figures following, to wit:

Filed Sep 1932.

87   * * (Caption) * *

PETITION FOR APPEAL.

To the Honorable Walter C. Lindley, Judge of the United States District Court:

L. J. Bosworth, Receiver of McCartney National Bank of Green Bay, Wisconsin, your petitioner, who is the plaintiff in the above entitled cause, prays that he may be permitted to take an appeal from the judgment entered in the above cause on the 6th day of August, 1932, to the United States Circuit Court of Appeals for the Seventh Circuit for the reasons specified in the Assignment of Errors which is filed herewith.

Your petitioner represents that this appeal is requested at the direction of the Comptroller of the Currency of United States and pursuant to the statute no bond or security should be required.

Wherefore your petitioner prays that an order be made allowing said appeal without bond.

MILLER, GORHAM, WALES & ADAMS
Attorneys for Plaintiff.

88   And on, to wit, the 30th day of September, 1932 came
    the Plaintiff by his attorneys and filed in the Clerk's
office of said Court a certain Assignment of Errors in words
and figures following, to wit:

89   * * (Caption) * *

ASSIGNMENT OF ERRORS.

Comes now the said L. J. Bosworth, Receiver of The Mc-
Cartney National Bank of Green Bay, Wisconsin, plaintiff in
the above entitled cause, and files the assignment of errors
on which he will rely in the prosecution of the appeal herewith petitioned for in said cause from the judgment of this
Court entered on the 6th day of August, 1932.

1.   The Court erred in entering judgment for the defendant.

2.   The court erred in not entering judgment for the plaintiff.

3.   The court erred in finding the issues for the defendant.

4.   The court erred in not finding the issues for the plaintiff.

5.   The court erred in holding the defendant had a claim
which it was entitled to set off against the plaintiff's cause
    of action.

90   6.   The Court erred in not holding that the defendant
    had no claim of any character which it was entitled to
set off against the plaintiff's cause of action.

7.   The Court erred in denying the motion of the plaintiff
to find the issues in favor of the plaintiff and to enter judgment accordingly.

8.   The Court erred in not granting the motion of the plaintiff to find the issues in favor of the plaintiff and to enter
judgment accordingly.

9.   The Court erred in admitting evidence on behalf of the
defendant that the defendant had debited the account of The
McCartney National Bank after learning of its insolvency
and in admitting defendant's Exhibit 1 constituting the debit
memorandum made by the defendant against the account of
The McCartney National Bank after learning of the latter's
insolvency in the amount of the items forwarded to that bank
May 26, 1931; and the Court erred in denying the motion of
plaintiff to strike said evidence and in not striking said evi-

dence and said Exhibit on the ground that they were immaterial.

10. The Court erred in admitting evidence on behalf of the defendant as to the character of the endorsements on the items forwarded by the defendant to The McCartney National Bank; and the Court erred in denying the motion of the plaintiff to strike said evidence on the ground that said evidence was not the best evidence and on the further ground that said evidence was immaterial.

11. The Court erred in denying the motion of the plaintiff requesting the Court to find that the defendant was not the owner of the items which it forwarded to The Mc-

91   Cartney National Bank May 26, 1931, nor of any credit arising by the receipt and acceptance of said items by The McCartney National Bank.

12. The Court erred in denying the motion of the plaintiff requesting the Court to find that the defendant was not the beneficial owner of the items which it forwarded to The McCartney National Bank May 26, 1931, nor of any credit arising by the receipt and acceptance of said items by The McCartney National Bank.

13. The Court erred in denying the motion of the plaintiff requesting the Court to find that the defendant was not the owner of the draft issued by The McCartney National Bank May 27, 1931 and received by the defendant May 28, 1931.

14. The Court erred in denying the motion of the plaintiff requesting the Court to find that the defendant was not the beneficial owner of the draft issued by The McCartney National Bank May 27, 1931 and received by the defendant May 28, 1931.

15. There was no evidence sufficient in law to support the second finding of fact, and the Court erred in making said second finding of fact, as follows, to wit:

"The Court finds that each, every and all of said checks drawn on the McCartney National Bank which were forwarded by the defendant Bank to the McCartney National Bank on May 26, 1931, for collection and returns in Chicago exchange were endorsed: 'Pay to the order of Continental-Illinois Bank and Trust Company' or 'Pay to the order of any bank, banker or trust company'."

92   16. There was no evidence sufficient in law to support the finding of fact, and the Court erred in making said third finding of fact, as follows, to-wit:

"The Court finds that the defendant on May 28, 1931, which was after it learned that the McCartney National Bank was closed, made a debit memorandum debiting the account of the McCartney National Bank with the total amount of the items which were forwarded by the defendant to the McCartney National Bank on May 26, 1931."

17. The findings of fact were insufficient to support a judgment for the defendant, and the Court erred in entering judgment for the defendant on the basis of said findings.

18. The findings of the court were insufficient to support the conclusion that the defendant had a claim which it was entitled to set off against the plaintiff's cause of action, and the Court erred in holding that the defendant had such a claim on the basis of its findings.

19. The court erred in denying plaintiff's motion for a new trial.

20. The court erred in denying the plaintiff's motion in arrest of judgment.

Wherefore, Plaintiff prays that the said judgment may be reversed and for such other and further relief as to the court may seem just and proper.

MILLER, GORHAM, WALES & ADAMS,
Attorneys for Plaintiff.

Dated: Sept. 29, 1932.

red Sept.
1932.

93   And afterwards, to wit, on the 30th day of September, 1932 being one of the days of the regular September term of said Court, in the record of proceedings thereof, in said entitled cause, before the Honorable Walter C. Lindley, District Judge, appears the following entry, to wit:

94   * * (Caption) * *

ORDER.

The petition of L. J. Bosworth, Receiver of McCartney National Bank of Green Bay, Wisconsin, plaintiff in the above entitled cause, for an appeal from the final judgment herein, is hereby granted and the appeal to the United States Circuit Court of Appeals for the Seventh Circuit is allowed.

And it appearing to the Court that said appeal was taken at the direction of the Comptroller of the Currency of the United States;

It is further Ordered that no bond or scurity be required on said appeal.

Enter:

WALTER C. LINDLEY,
District Judge.

Dated, Sept. 30, 1932.

58   And on, to wit, the 26th day of August, 1932 came the Plaintiff by his attorneys and filed in the Clerk's office of said Court a certain Notice in words and figures following, to wit: Filed Aug 1932.

59   * * (Caption) * *

NOTICE.

To: Mayer, Meyer, Austrian and Platt
    Attorneys for Defendant
       231 South LaSalle Street
       Chicago, Illinois

Please Take Notice, That the plaintiff will on Friday, August 26, 1932, at the hour of 10 A. M. or as soon thereafter as counsel may be heard, move the Honorable Walter C. Lindley, Judge of the United States District Court in the City of Chicago, for an order extending the time of the plaintiff within which to prepare, file and serve the bill of exceptions in the above entitled case thirty (30) days from September 3, 1932, to and including October 3, 1932.

MILLER, GORHAM, WALES & ADAMS,
Attorneys for Plaintiff.

Received a copy of the above and foregoing notice, together with a copy of the order therein mentioned, this 25th day of August, A. D. 1932.

MAYER, MEYER, AUSTRIAN & PLATT.

60   And on, to wit, the 26th day of August, 1932 came the
Plaintiff by his attorneys and filed in the Clerk's office
of said Court a certain Motion in words and figures following, to wit:

61   ·   * * (Caption) * *

MOTION FOR EXTENSION OF TIME TO FILE BILL OF EXCEPTIONS.

Now comes the plaintiff, L. J. Bosworth, Receiver of The
McCartney National Bank of Green Bay, Wisconsin, and
shows to the Court that this term of court adjourns September 3, 1932; that additional time is needed within which to
prepare and file a bill of exceptions herein.

Wherefore, plaintiff prays for an extension of thirty (30)
days from and after September 3, 1932, within which to prepare, have allowed and file said bill of exceptions, said extension to have the same force and effect as if the present term
of Court continued throughout said thirty (30) day period.

MILLER, GORHAM, WALES & ADAMS,
Attorneys for L. J. Bosworth, Receiver of
The McCartney National Bank of Green
Bay, Wisconsin.

ered Aug.
1932.

62   And afterwards, to wit, on the 26th day of August,
1932, being one of the days of the regular July term of
said Court, in the record of proceedings thereof, in said entitled cause, before the Honorable Walter C. Lindley, District
Judge, appears the following entry, to wit:

63   * *(Caption) * *

ORDER.

On this 26th day of August, 1932, upon the motion of L.
J. Bosworth, Receiver of The McCartney National Bank of
Green Bay, Wisconsin, plaintiff in the above entitled cause,
good cause being shown therefore, the time for the signing,
allowance and filing of the bill of exceptions in the above
named case is hereby extended thirty (30) days from September 3, 1932, to and including October 3, 1932, and it is

further ordered that the present term of this Court be and the same hereby is extended for said purpose until the expiration of said extended time.

Enter:

WALTER C. LINDLEY
District Judge.

O. K.

MAYER, MEYER, AUSTRIAN & PLATT
Dated August 26th, 1932.

95   * * (Caption) * *

PRAECIPE FOR TRANSCRIPT OF RECORD.

To the Clerk of the United States District Court, Northern District of Illinois, Eastern Division:

You are hereby requested to make a transcript of the records and proceedings had in your court in the above entitled cause to be filed in the United States Circuit Court of Appeals for the Seventh Circuit, pursuant to an appeal allowed in the above cause, and to include in such transcript of record the following, towit:

1. Praecipe filed November 24, 1931.
2. Declaration filed November 24, 1931.
3. Summons of November 27, 1931, returned served on the defendant December 14, 1931.
4. Appearance of Continental-Illinois Bank and Trust Company, defendant, filed December 14, 1931.
5. Plea and affidavit of merits of the defendant filed December 30, 1931.
6. Stipulation waiving jury and submitting cause to court, filed June 7, 1932.
96   7. Plaintiff's and defendant's Exhibit 1, being a stipulation of facts filed June 7, 1932.
8. Plaintiff's and defendant's Exhibit 2, being an amendment to stipulation of facts filed June 7, 1932.
9. Defendant's Exhibit 1, being a debit memorandum filed June 7, 1932.
10. Motion to find issues in favor of plaintiff filed August 8, 1932.
11. Request of the defendant for findings filed August 8, 1932.
12. Motion of plaintiff for findings filed September 3, 1932.

13. Findings of the court dated August 6, 1932 entered September 3, 1932.

14. Memorandum of Judge Lindley filed August 6, 1932.

15. Judgment entered August 6, 1932 in favor of defendant against plaintiff, dismissing the suit with costs assessed against plaintiff.

16. Notice filed August 26, 1932.

17. Motion of plaintiff filed August 26, 1932 to extend time for allowance and filing bill of exceptions to October 3, 1932.

18. Order entered August 26, 1932, extending time for filing of bill of exceptions to October 3, 1932.

19. Notice filed Septemebr 30, 1932.

20. Petition for appeal and assignments of error filed September 30, 1932.

21. Order entered September 30, 1932, allowing appeal.

97   22. Original bill of exceptions filed September 30, 1932.

23. This praecipe and service thereon.

Said transcript to be prepared as required by law and the rules of this court and the rules of the United States Circuit Court of Appeals for the Seventh Circuit, and to be filed in the office of the Clerk of the United States Court of Appeals, Seventh Circuit, at Chicago on or before the 29th day of October, 1932.

MILLER, GORHAM, WALES & ADAMS
Attorneys for Appellant, L. J. Bosworth, Receiver.

Service of the above praecipe accepted and acknowledged this 7th day of October, 1932.

MAYER, MEYER, AUSTRIAN & PLATT
Attorneys for Appellee, Continental Illinois Bank and Trust Company.

98 Northern District of Illinois } ss.
      Eastern Division

I, Charles M. Bates, Clerk of the District Court of the United States for the Northern District of Illinois, do hereby certify the above and foregoing to be a true and complete transcript of the proceedings had of record made in accordance with Praecipe filed in this Court in the cause entitled L. J. Bosworth, Receiver of McCartney National Bank of Green Bay, Wisconsin *vs.* Continental-Illinois Bank and Trust Company, a corp., No. 40116, as the same appear from the original records and files thereof now remaining in my custody and control.

In Testimony Whereof, I have hereunto set my hand and affixed the seal of said Court at my office, in the City of Chicago, in said District, this 3rd day of November, A. D. 1932.

                              CHARES M. BATES

(Seal)   *Clerk.*

99 United States } ss.
     of America,

The President of the United States, To Continental-Illinois Bank and Trust Company, a corporation, Greeting:

You are hereby cited and admonished to be and appear at a United States Circuit Court of Appeals, for the Seventh Circuit, to be holden at Chicago, within thirty days from the date hereof, pursuant to an order of September 30, 1932 allowing an appeal filed in the Clerk's Office of the District Court of the United States for the Northern District of Illinois, Eastern Division, wherein L. J. Bosworth, Receiver of The McCartney National Bank of Green Bay, Wisconsin, is appellant, and you are appellee, to show cause, if any there be, why the judgment rendered against the said appellant as in the said appeal mentioned, should not be corrected and why speedy justice should not be done to the parties in that behalf.

Witness the Honorable Walter C. Lindley Judge of the District Court of the United States, this fifth day of October, in the year of our Lord one thousand nine hundred and thirty-two.

                            WALTER C. LINDLEY

                                Judge

On this 7th day of October, in the year of our Lord one thousand nine hundred and thirty-two, personally appeared John Brosnahan before me, the subscriber, a Notary Public in and for Cook County, Illinois, and makes oath that he delivered a true copy of the within citation to Frank Mayer.

Sworn to and subscribed the 7th day of October, A. D. 1932.

SYDNEY CORRIGAN

(Seal)

(Endorsed) * * (Caption) * * Citation. Filed Oct 7-1932 Charles M. Bates, Clerk.

UNITED STATES CIRCUIT COURT OF APPEALS

For the Seventh Circuit.

———

I, Frederick G. Campbell, Clerk of the United States Circuit Court of Appeals for the Seventh Circuit, do hereby certify that the foregoing Printed Pages, numbered from 1 to 44, inclusive, contain a true copy of the Printed Record, printed under my supervision and filed on the twenty-eighth day of December, 1932, on which the following entitled cause was heard and determined:

L. J. Bosworth, Receiver of The McCartney National Bank of Green Bay, Wisconsin,
Appellant,

vs.

Continental Illinois Bank & Trust Co.,
Appellee,

No. 4887, October Term, 1932, as the same remains upon the files and records of the United States Circuit Court of Appeals for the Seventh Circuit.

In Testimony Whereof I hereunto subscribe my name and affix the seal of said United States Circuit Court of Appeals for the Seventh Circuit, at the City of Chicago, this 26 day of July, A. D. 1933.

FREDERICK G. CAMPBELL,
Clerk of the United States Circuit Court of Appeals for the Seventh Circuit.

(Seal)

At a regular term of the United States Circuit Court of Appeals for the Seventh Circuit begun and held in the United States Court Room in the City of Chicago, in said Seventh Circuit, on the fourth day of October, 1932, of the October Term, in the year of our Lord One Thousand Nine Hundred and Thirty-two, and of our Independence the One Hundred and Fifty-Seventh.

L. J. Bosworth, Receiver, Etc., 4887   *vs.* Continental Illinois Bank & Trust Co.

Appeal from the District Court of the United States for the Northern District of Illinois, Eastern Division.

And afterwards, to-wit: On the twenty-first day of November, 1932, there was filed in the Office of the Clerk of this Court an Appearance of counsel for Appellant, which said Appearance is in the words and figures following, to-wit:

UNITED STATES CIRCUIT COURT OF APPEALS

For the Seventh Circuit.

No. 4887.   October Term, 1932.

L. J. Bosworth, Receiver of the McCartney National Bank of Green Bay, Wisconsin,

Appellant,

vs.

Continental Illinois Bank and Trust Company, a Corporation,

Appellee.

The Clerk will enter my appearance as Counsel for Appellant.

AMOS C. MILLER,
HENRY W. WALES,
    One La Salle St.,
    Chicago, Illinois.

Endorsed: Filed November 21, 1932. Frederick G. Campbell, Clerk.

And on the same day, to-wit: On the twenty-first day of November, 1932, the following further proceedings were had and entered of record, to-wit:

Monday, November 21, 1932.

Court met pursuant to adjournment and was opened by proclamation.

Present:

Hon. Samuel Alschuler, Circuit Judge, presiding.
Hon. William M. Sparks, Circuit Judge.
Frederick G. Campbell, Clerk.
Henry C. W. Laubenheimer, Marshal.

Before:

Hon. William M. Sparks, Circuit Judge.

L. J. Bosworth, Receiver, Etc., 4887 *vs.* Continental Illinois Bank & Trust Co.	Appeal from the District Court of the United States for the Northern District of Illinois, Eastern Division.

On motion of Miller, Gorham, Wales and Adams, Attorneys for appellant, and good and sufficient cause having been shown, it is ordered that the appeal in this cause be docketed instanter, and that the transcript of record from the District Court of the United States for the Northern District of Illinois, Eastern Division, be filed instanter with the Clerk of this Court.

And afterwards, to-wit: On the twenty-fifth day of November, 1932, there was filed in the office of the Clerk of this Court, an appearance of counsel for appellee, which said appearance is in the words and figures following, to-wit:

UNITED STATES CIRCUIT COURT OF APPEALS

For the Seventh Circuit.

No. 4887.   October Term, 1932.

L. J. Bosworth, Receiver of the McCartney National Bank of
Green Bay, Wisconsin,
Appellant,

vs.

Continental Illinois Bank and Trust Company, a Corporation,
Appellee.

The Clerk will enter our Appearance as counsel for appellee.

CARL MEYER,
FRANK D. MAYER,
231 So. La Salle St.,
Chicago, Illinois.

Endorsed: Filed November 25, 1932. Frederick G. Campbell, Clerk.

And afterwards, to-wit: On the thirtieth day of November, 1932, there was filed in the office of the Clerk of this Court an appearance of counsel for appellant, which said appearance is in the words and figures following, to-wit:

UNITED STATES CIRCUIT COURT OF APPEALS

For the Seventh Circuit.

No. 4887.   October Term, 1932.

L. J. Bosworth, Receiver of the McCartney National Bank of
Green Bay, Wisconsin,
Appellant,

vs.

Continental Illinois Bank and Trust Company, a Corporation,
Appellee.

The Clerk will enter our appearance as counsel for appellant.

SIDNEY S. GORHAM,
EDWARD R. ADAMS,
One La Salle Street,
Chicago, Illinois.

Endorsed: Filed November 30, 1932. Frederick G. Campbell, Clerk.

———————

And afterwards, to-wit: On the first day of December, 1932, there was filed in the office of the Clerk of this Court, a Stipulation with Reference to the Printing of the Record, which Stipulation is in the words and figures following, to-wit:

United States ⎰ ss.
 of America, ⎱

IN THE UNITED STATES CIRCUIT COURT OF APPEALS

For the Seventh Circuit.

L. J. Bosworth, Receiver for The
  McCartney National Bank of
  Green Bay, Wisconsin,
                    Appellant,
        vs.   ⎰ No. 4887.
Continental Illinois Bank and
  Trust Company, a corporation,
                    Appellee.

STIPULATION.

It is Stipulated and Agreed by and between the parties hereto, by their respective attorneys, that in printing the transcript of record herein the stipulation of facts, amendment to stipulation and debit memorandum filed in the District Court August 6, 1932, and introduced in evidence on the trial of this cause in the District Colrt, and included in the transcript of record herein, may be omitted, except as the same may appear as a part of the bill of exceptions, provided, however, that the printed transcript of record shall contain appropriate notations, showing such omissions and designating by appropriate references to the pages in the printed transcript of record, where such documents may be found printed as a part of the bill of exceptions.

It is further agreed that at any time hereafter either party may cause such omissions, or any thereof, to be printed and filed herein, with the same effect as if they had originally appeared in said printed transcript of record.

MILLER, GORHAM, WALES AND ADAMS,
        Attorneys for Plaintiff-Appellant.
MAYER, MEYER, AUSTRIAN & PLATT,
        Attorneys for Defendant-Appellee.

Endorsed: Filed December 1, 1932. Frederick G. Campbell, Clerk.

And afterwards, to-wit: On the eleventh day of April, 1933, the following further proceedings were had and entered of record, to-wit:

Tuesday, April 11, 1933.

Court met pursuant to adjournment and was opened by proclamation.

Present:

Hon. Samuel Alschuler, Circuit Judge, presiding.
Hon. Evan A. Evans, Circuit Judge.
Hon. William M. Sparks, Circuit Judge.
Hon. Robert C. Baltzell, District Judge.
Frederick G. Campbell, Clerk.
Henry C. W. Laubenheimer, Marshal.

Before:

Hon. Evan A. Evans, Circuit Judge.
Hon. William M. Sparks, Circuit Judge.
Hon. Robert C. Baltzell, District Judge.

L. J. Bosworth, Receiver, 4887 *vs.* Continental Illinois Bank & Trust Co.	Appeal from the District Court of the United States for the Northern District of Illinois, Eastern Division.

It is ordered by the Court that this cause be, and the same is hereby set down for hearing on May 12, 1933.

———————

And afterwards, to-wit: On the twelfth day of May, 1933, the following further proceedings were had and entered of record, to-wit:

Friday, May 12, 1933.

Court met pursuant to adjournment and was opened by proclamation.

Present:

Hon. Samuel Alschuler, Circuit Judge, presiding.
Hon. Evan A. Evans, Circuit Judge.
Hon. William M. Sparks, Circuit Judge.
Hon. George A. Carpenter, District Judge.
Frederick G. Campbell, Clerk.
Henry C. W. Laubenheimer, Marshal.

Before:

Hon. Samuel Alschuler, Circuit Judge.
Hon. Evan A. Evans, Circuit Judge.
Hon. George A. Carpenter, District Judge.

L. J. Bosworth, Receiver, 4887 *vs.* Continental Illinois Bank & Trust Co.	Appeal from the District Court of the United States for the Northern District of Illinois, Eastern Division.

Now this day comes the parties by their counsel and this cause now comes on to be heard on the printed record and briefs of counsel and on oral arguments by Mr. Robert W. Wales, counsel for appellant, and by Mr. Frank D. Mayer, counsel for appellee, and the court having heard the same takes this matter under advisement.

———

And afterwards, to-wit: On the fifth day of June, 1933, there was filed in the office of the Clerk of this Court, the Opinion of the Court, which said Opinion is in the words and figures following, to-wit:

In the United States Circuit Court of Appeals

For the Seventh Circuit.

No. 4887.   October Term, 1932, April Session, 1933.

L. J. BOSWORTH, Receiver of THE Mc-CARTNEY NATIONAL BANK OF GREEN BAY, WISCONSIN, *Appellant,* *vs.* CONTINENTAL ILLINOIS BANK AND TRUST COMPANY, a Corporation, *Appellee.*	Appeal from the District Court of the United States for the Northern District of Illinois, Eastern Division.

June 5, 1933.

Before Alschuler and Evans, *Circuit Judges*, and Carpenter, *District Judge*.

Evans, *Circuit Judge*. A single question, which is both close and interesting, is presented by this appeal. It concerns the right of a bank to set off against a deposit the amount of checks by it received shortly before the drawee bank closed its doors.

The facts: Appellant, receiver of the McCartney National Bank of Green Bay, Wisconsin, sued appellee to recover the amount the McCartney National Bank had on deposit when it closed. Appellee refused payment because it had applied the sum on deposit in partial satisfaction of a debt alleged to be due it.

On May 26, 1931, appellee received from its depositors, checks drawn on the McCartney National Bank, aggregating $10,823.14. These checks were forwarded to the McCartney National Bank where they arrived May 27, and the accounts of the drawers of the checks were duly charged with the amounts of the checks by them drawn. On the same day, the McCartney National Bank sent its draft for $10,823.14 on the Federal Reserve Bank of Chicago to appellee. That evening, and before appellee received the draft, the McCartney National Bank closed. The next morning the Federal Reserve Bank refused to pay the draft. Appellee applied the amount of the McCartney National Bank's deposit with it toward the payment of the draft.

When appellee received the one hundred twenty-two checks drawn on the McCartney National Bank on May 26, it credited each depositor's account with the amount of the checks deposited. When the McCartney National Bank's draft was refused payment by the Federal Reserve Bank, appellee promptly charged each depositor's account with the amounts previously credited. Between the date of the deposit and the date of the charge back, no depositor had withdrawn any of the sum thus credited to his account.

The canceled checks were never returned to appellee, but were delivered to the respective makers by the receiver of the McCartney National Bank.

Appellee received the checks and deposited the amount thereof to the depositor's account pursuant to an agreement, portions of which are herewith quoted:

"In receiving and handling items for deposit or collection (including items received in payment of collections) this Bank acts only as depositor's collecting agent and assumes no responsibility beyond the exercise of due care. *All items are credited or cashed subject to final payment in cash or solvent credits.* This Bank will not be liable for default or negligence of its correspondents, nor for losses in transit, and no correspondent shall be liable except for its own negligence. It is optional but not obligatory, to request certification in any case. This Bank or its correspondents may, as depositor's agent, send items, directly or indirectly, to any bank or to any drawee, acceptor or payor, and accept draft, check or credit as conditional payment in lieu of cash. It may charge back any item at any time before final payment, whether returned or not, also any item drawn on this Bank not good at close of business on day deposited. It may decline to honor or pay checks drawn against conditional credits. This Bank shall have a lien on all items handled by it and on the proceeds thereof for its charges, expenses (including court costs and attorney's fees) and any advances made by it in connection therewith."

All of the checks were forwarded by appellee to the McCartney National Bank for collection and return in Chicago exchange and were either endorsed: "Pay to the order of Continental Illinois Bank and Trust Company" or "Pay to the order of any bank, banker, or trust company."

The determinative question may be stated thus: When the payees named in the checks drawn on the McCartney National Bank endorsed them and appellee credited the depositors' accounts with the amounts thereof, did there arise such a debtor-creditor relationship between the McCartney National Bank and appellee as to permit the latter to apply the former's deposit in extinction of the debt?

Appellant answers this question in the negative, relying upon the agreement between appellee and its depositor which expressly provided that "all items are credited or cashed subject to final payment in cash or solvent credits" and "in receiving and handling items for deposit or collection * * * this Bank acts only as depositor's collecting agent and assumes no responsibility beyond the exercise of due care" and the bank "may charge back any item at any time before final payment, whether returned or not, also any item drawn on this Bank not good at close of business on day deposited."

Briefly stated, it is appellant's position that appellee was but an agent of the payees named in the checks, to collect the amounts thereof; that no such title ever passed to appellee as to permit it to set off as against the amounts due on the said checks the amount which the McCartney National Bank had on deposit with appellee.

It seems to us that appellant overemphasizes the written agreement above referred to, the purpose and object of which was to limit the liability of the bank to its depositors, and ignores the legal consequences which resulted from the unqualified endorsement of the checks. While the agreement between appellee and its depositors gave to the bank the right to recharge the depositors' accounts with the amounts of the checks in case the latter were not paid, and placed a limitation or restriction on the bank's liability to its depositors, it would hardly be fair to look solely to this document to determine whether appellee, as against the McCartney National Bank, was a creditor.

The court can not, and should not, overlook the acts of the parties accompanying the transaction, nor can we ignore the unqualified endorsements which the payees of the checks wrote upon the back of them. These endorsements, unexplained, gave to appellee the right to maintain an action against the McCartney National Bank upon those checks, if they were not paid when presented.

Such a right as against the McCartney National Bank would not defeat nor destroy appellee's right to look also to the endorsers of the checks. Appellee had two remedies if the checks were unpaid. It could sue the McCartney National Bank, and it could pursue the endorser who endorsed the check. The existence of the one remedy was not inconsistent with the other. Appellee's liability to its endorser might be measured by that of an agent to its principal and yet such a transfer of interest occur through payees' unqualified endorsement and by the transfer of money by the bank to the accounts of the payees as to make the bank a creditor with right to sue the drawee bank upon nonpayment of the checks.

Several very recent decisions dealing with somewhat similar fact situations have been called to our attention, and they are favorable to appellee. *A. M. Anderson, Receiver,* v. *Taver Bayly,* decided March 4, 1933 (CCA 5); *Harold Nomland, Receiver,* v. *First National Bank of Kansas City,* filed April 3, 1933 (CCA 8).

Counsel for appellant has pointed out the differences in the agreements (banks' agreements with depositors), and thereby seeks to distinguish the holdings. We must admit, of course, that the terms of the agreements between depositors and banks are not identical in the cited cases with the agreement in this case. But the reasoning which led to the conclusions reached makes such differences non-essential.

Moreover in the instant case, appellee's claim to be the creditor of the McCartney National Bank at the time it applied the latter's deposit to a satisfaction of the claim was greatly strengthened and fortified by the action of the McCartney National Bank upon the receipt of the checks from appellee. The McCartney National Bank, immediately upon receiving the checks from appellee, charged each of its customers with the amount of the check by him drawn. It then executed its draft on the Federal Reserve Bank of Chicago, payable to appellee, and mailed it to appellee. Thus it will be seen that when appellee applied the deposit of the McCartney National Bank to the extinguishment of its debts, its position as a *creditor* was no longer dependent solely on the transfer of checks, but its creditor position rested upon (a) the endorsement of checks to appellee, (b) the crediting of appellee's depositors' accounts with the amount thereof, (c) the issuance of a draft by the McCartney National Bank to appellee, and (d) the charging of the account of the de-

positors of the McCartney National Bank with the amount
of the checks for which that bank sent appellee its draft.

The judgment is

AFFIRMED.

Endorsed: Filed June 5, 1933. Frederick G. Campbell,
Clerk.

And on the same day, to-wit: On the fifth day of June,
1933, the following further proceedings were had and entered
of record, to-wit:

Monday, June 5, 1933.

Court met pursuant to adjournment and was opened by
proclamation.

Present:

      Hon. Samuel Alschuler, Circuit Judge, presiding.
      Hon. Evan A. Evans, Circuit Judge.
      Hon. William M. Sparks, Circuit Judge.
        Frederick G. Campbell, Clerk.
        Henry C. W. Laubenheimer, Marshal.

Before:

      Hon. Samuel Alschuler, Circuit Judge.
      Hon. Evan A. Evans, Circuit Judge.
      Hon. George A. Carpenter, District Judge.

L. J. Bosworth, Receiver, etc., 4887 *vs.* Continental Illinois Bank & Trust Co.	Appeal from the District Court of the United States for the Northern District of Illinois, Eastern Division.

This cause came on to be heard on the transcript of the
record from the District Court of the United States for the
Northern District of Illinois, Eastern Division, and was ar-
gued by counsel.

On consideration whereof: It is now here ordered and ad-
judged by this Court that the judgment of the said District
Court in this cause be, and the same is hereby affirmed with
costs.

And afterwards, to-wit: On the twenty-sixth day of June, 1933, the Mandate of this Court issued to the District Court of the United States for the Northern District of Illinois, Eastern Division.

———

And afterwards, to-wit: On the twenty-seventh day of June, 1933, there was filed in the office of the Clerk of this Court, a Motion to recall and stay the Mandate, which said Motion is in the words and figures following, to-wit:

UNITED STATES CIRCUIT COURT OF APPEALS

For the Seventh Circuit.

L. J. Bosworth, Receiver,	
v.	No. 4887.
Continental Illinois Bank & Trust Company.	

MOTION.

Now comes L. J. Bosworth, Receiver, appellant, by Henry W. Wales, his attorney, and moves the Court to recall the mandate issued in the above entitled cause and to stay the issuance of any mandate for thirty (30) days pending the determination of whether certiorari from the United States Supreme Court will be asked.

HENRY W. WALES,
Attorney for Appellant.

Endorsed: Filed June 27, 1933. Frederick G. Campbell, Clerk.

———

And on the same day, to-wit: On the twenty-seventh day of June, 1933, the following further proceedings were had and entered of record, to-wit:

Tuesday, June 27, 1933.

Court met pursuant to adjournment and was opened by proclamation.

Present:

Hon. Samuel Alschuler, Circuit Judge.
Hon. Evan A. Evans, Circuit Judge.
Hon. William M. Sparks, Circuit Judge.
Frederick G. Campbell, Clerk.
Henry C. W. Laubenheimer, Marshal.

Before:

Hon. Samuel Alschuler, Circuit Judge.

| L. J. Bosworth, Receiver, 4887 *vs.* Continental Illinois Bank & Trust Co. | Appeal from the District Court of the United States for the Northern District of Illinois, Eastern Division. |

Now this day comes counsel for appellant and presents a motion for the recall and stay of the Mandate of this Court pending a petition to the Supreme Court of the United States for a writ of certiorari.

On consideration whereof: It is now here ordered that the Mandate in this cause be, and the same is hereby recalled and stayed until the further order of this Court.

It is further ordered that Counsel for appellant proceed with diligence and promptly file the petition for a writ of certiorari in the Supreme Court of the United States and, upon the filing of said petition file in this Court proof of the filing of said petition in said Court.

UNITED STATES CIRCUIT COURT OF APPEALS

For the Seventh Circuit.

I, Frederick G. Campbell, Clerk of the United States Circuit Court of Appeals for the Seventh Circuit, do hereby certify that the foregoing printed pages, numbered from 47 to 60, inclusive, contain a true copy of the proceedings had and papers filed (except the Briefs of Counsel, and orders relating to the filing of briefs) in the case of

L. J. Bosworth, Receiver of The McCartney National Bank of Green Bay, Wisconsin,

Appellant,

vs.

Continental Illinois Bank & Trust Co.,

Appellee,

No. 4887, October Term, 1932, as the same remains upon the files and records of the United States Circuit Court of Appeals for the Seventh Circuit.

In Testimony Whereof I hereunto subscribe my name and affix the seal of said United States Circuit Court of Appeals for the Seventh Circuit, at the City of Chicago, this 26 day of July, A. D. 1933.

FREDERICK G. CAMPBELL,

(Seal)

Clerk of the United States Circuit Court of Appeals for the Seventh Circuit.

SUPREME COURT OF THE UNITED STATES

ORDER ALLOWING CERTIORARI—Filed December 4, 1933

The petition herein for a writ of certiorari to the United States Circuit Court of Appeals for the Seventh Circuit is granted. And it is further ordered that the duly certified copy of the transcript of the proceedings below which accompanied the petition shall be treated as though filed in response to such writ.

(4321)

IN THE

Supreme Court of the United States

OCTOBER TERM, A. D. 1933.

No. 358

L. J. BOSWORTH, RECEIVER OF THE McCARTNEY NATIONAL
BANK OF GREEN BAY, WISCONSIN,

Petitioner,

vs.

CONTINENTAL ILLINOIS BANK AND TRUST
COMPANY,

Respondent.

BRIEF OF PETITIONER.

AMOS C. MILLER,
SIDNEY S. GORHAM,
HENRY W. WALES,
EDWARD R. ADAMS,
Counsel for Petitioner.

F. G. AWALT,
GEORGE P. BARSE,
JOHN F. ANDERSON,
GEORGE B. SPRINGSTON,
Attorneys for Comptroller
of the Currency,
Of Counsel.

THE GUNTHORP-WARREN PRINTING COMPANY, 210 WEST JACKSON, CHICAGO

INDEX.

Table of Cases.

IN THE

Supreme Court of the United States

OCTOBER TERM, A. D. 1933.

No. 358

L. J. BOSWORTH, RECEIVER OF THE McCARTNEY NATIONAL
BANK OF GREEN BAY, WISCONSIN,

Petitioner,

vs.

CONTINENTAL ILLINOIS BANK AND TRUST
COMPANY,

Respondent.

BRIEF OF PETITIONER.

DECISIONS BELOW.

The opinion of the Circuit Court of Appeals for the
Seventh Circuit is reported in 65 F. (2d) 632. It is set
forth on page 54 of the record. The memorandum opinion of the District Court has not been officially reported;
it appears on page 14 of the record.

JURISDICTION.

Certiorari was granted by this Court December 4,
1933.

STATEMENT OF THE CASE.

This action was brought by L. J. Bosworth, as Receiver of the insolvent The McCartney National Bank, to recover the amount on deposit with the respondent bank, Continental Illinois Bank and Trust Company, to the credit of the insolvent bank. The respondent (defendant below) resisted the action on the ground that it had the right to set off against the amount of the deposit a sum representing the amount of certain checks forwarded by the respondent to the insolvent bank prior to its closing. The case was heard on two stipulations of fact (R. 22-27) and a small amount of additional testimony introduced by the respondent. (R. 28-29) The trial court, sitting without a jury, allowed the set-off and entered judgment for the defendant. (R. 21; Memorandum Opinion, R. 14). The Circuit Court of Appeals for the Seventh Circuit affirmed the judgment. (R. 58; Opinion, R. 54, reported 65 F. (2d) 632).

Customers of the Continental Bank (the respondent) delivered to it checks drawn on The McCartney National Bank. The checks were received by the respondent under a written contract (set forth in full in the Appendix hereof, and in the Record on page 25) which expressly provided that the Continental Bank

> "acts only as depositor's collecting agent and assumes no responsibility beyond the exercise of due care. All items are credited or cashed subject to final payment in cash or solvent credits." (R. 25)

The agreement also provided that

> "This Bank or its correspondents may, as depositor's agent, send items, directly or indirectly, to any bank or to any drawee, acceptor or payor, and accept draft, check or credit as conditional payment in lieu of cash." (R. 25)

Upon receipt of these checks the respondent credited the amounts thereof to its respective depositors (R. 23), but these credits were not altered by withdrawals, over-drafts, or otherwise, between the time of credit and the moment respondent charged the items back against its customers as hereafter described. (R. 26) The respondent forwarded the checks to The McCartney National Bank on May 26, 1931, for collection and returns in Chicago Exchange. (R. 23) Upon receipt thereof the following day The McCartney National Bank charged the checks to the respective accounts of its customers who had issued them and mailed to the respondent its draft on the Federal Reserve Bank of Chicago for the total amount of the checks. (R. 23)

The McCartney National Bank suspended the evening of May 27, 1931. (R. 23) The next morning, the respondent received the draft sent it by The McCartney National Bank and presented it to the Federal Reserve Bank of Chicago before 10:30 A. M., but payment was refused since prior to the presentation of the draft the Federal Reserve Bank of Chicago had been notified of the closing of The McCartney National Bank. At 11:15 that morning the respondent was notified by telegram that The McCartney National Bank had suspended (R. 24), and thereafter respondent charged the McCartney Bank's credit balance with respondent with the amount of the checks forwarded. (R. 28) On May 29th and days following respondent charged back to the accounts of its customers the amounts of the checks drawn on The McCartney National Bank which had been deposited by them and duly notified its customers of this action. (R. 26)

At the trial the respondent introduced testimony subject to the objection of the petitioner that the checks so forwarded to The McCartney National Bank were endorsed "Pay to the order of Continental Illinois Bank and Trust Company," or "Pay to the order of any bank, banker or trust company." (R. 29) The petitioner's objection was that the oral testimony of the respondent's employee was not the best evidence of the nature of the endorsements, since the written documents should be produced. (R. 29) Furthermore, the evidence was impeached by the employee's statement that his testimony was based not on any particular recollection of the matter, but on the general custom, which was possibly not always followed. (R. 29)

By agreed adjustment of the accounts (R. 27) petitioner is entitled to recover the sum of $5,890.79, together with interest thereon, if allowable by law, unless the respondent is entitled to set off the amount of the checks forwarded under the above circumstances.

SPECIFICATION OF ERRORS.

1. The Court erred in holding that the defendant might set off an amount not beneficially owned by it, against the amount owed by it to the plaintiff by reason of the deposit of The McCartney National Bank in the defendant.

2. The Court erred in holding that ownership of the collection items involved passed to the defendant sufficiently to allow a set-off.

3. The Court erred in allowing the defendant to set off the amount of the collection items involved.

4. The Court erred in holding that the allowance of the set-off did not result in an unlawful preference to the defendant's customers, as owners of the collection items involved.

5. The Court erred in affirming the judgment for the defendant.

SUMMARY OF ARGUMENT.

1. This Court has held that a defendant when sued upon an individual debt may not set off a demand against the plaintiff held by the defendant in a fiduciary capacity. 2. The checks received by the respondent from its customers were held by it as agent under the terms of a written contract between the respondent and its customers. The beneficial ownership of the items remained in the customers until collection of such items was made in cash or solvent credits, which was never accomplished. Therefore, The McCartney National Bank's draft received by the respondent was likewise held as agent and beneficially owned by the respondent's customers. The set-off claimed by the respondent is thus asserted in an agency capacity and the debts between the banks not being held in the same right lack mutuality. 3. The National Bank Act requires a ratable distribution of the assets of an insolvent national bank. This purpose would be defeated and an illegal preference would be obtained by the customers of the respondent if the set-off claimed were allowed.

ARGUMENT.

Respondent is attempting to defeat the claim of the petitioner to a sum admittedly due the petitioner by setting off the amount of certain items which the respondent held as collecting agent. In other words, the respondent seeks to set off, as against a sum it individually owes, an amount which was due it only in a fiduciary capacity. The set-off would result in the owners of the items, the customers of the respondent, obtaining full payment (or nearly so) of their claims by the use of a deposit indebtedness with which they had no connection.

The instant case is controlled by the decision in *Dakin* v. *Bayly*, 78 L. Ed. 95 (No. 44 in the October 1933 term, decided November 20, 1933), which held that true mutuality is required before a set-off may be allowed—that the respective demands must be beneficially owned by the same parties. The respondent, in waiving its right to reply to the petition for certiorari, stated that the *Dakin* case involved the same questions as this case. Since *Dakin* v. *Bayly* clearly recognizes the necessity for mutuality of demands, in the sense of being held in the same capacity, as a requisite for set-off, it is unnecessary to review the earlier decisions to the same effect. The decision reaffirms the doctrine which has been long followed by this court that to allow set-off the demands must be beneficially owned by the same parties. See *Central National Bank of Baltimore* v. *Connecticut Mutual Life Ins. Co.*, 104 U. S. 54; *Scammon* v. *Kimball*, 92 U. S. 362; *United States* v. *Butterworth-Judson Corp.*, 267 U. S. 387; *Libby* v. *Hopkins*, 104 U. S. 303; and *Hanover National Bank* v. *Suddath*, 215 U. S. 122.

In so far as the facts in the instant case differ from those in the *Dakin* case, they are stronger for the petitioner. In this case the collection items, and the dishonored draft forwarded in an attempt to cover the items, were beneficially owned by the customers of the respondent just as they were in the *Dakin* case. The agreement of the present respondent with its customers, made upon receipt of the items, was much more definite than the provisions of the Florida statute which was relied upon in the *Dakin* case. Here the parties expressly stipulated that the respondent was to act only as collecting agent—the relationship could hardly be more clearly expressed; in the case cited the relationship had to be spelled out of the presumption that the parties intended such relation because of a statute defining the bank's liabilities. In the *Dakin* case it was apparently conceded that the checks were endorsed without restriction; in the present suit there is weak and incompetent evidence that the endorsements were of that character. In any event, as recognized in the *Dakin* opinion, the character of the endorsements is immaterial where the parties have expressly agreed on the nature of the relationship. This was merely confirmation of statements to like effect in *Burton* v. *United States*, 196 U. S. 283, 297, and in *Douglas* v. *Federal Reserve Bank of Dallas*, 271 U. S. 489; and of applications of the principle in the Circuit Courts of Appeals. *Washington Loan & Banking Co.* v. *Fourth National Bank of Macon*, 38 F. (2d) 772 (C. C. A. 5th, 1930); *First National Bank of Denver* v. *Federal Reserve Bank*, 6 F. (2d) 339 (C. C. A. 8th, 1925). In the present case it appears that the respondent gave its customers credit for the items deposited; but it also appears that there were no withdrawals against these credits and that the items were charged back to the customers. (R. 26) The agreement of the respondent advised its customers that the respondent reserved the right to decline to honor or pay checks drawn against conditional credits. (R. 25) Such provisional credits do not render the bank owner. *St. Louis & San Francisco Railway* v. *Johnston*, 133 U. S. 566. In the *Dakin* case it did not appear whether the customers were given credit or whether the credits were of a provisional nature, yet the relationship was held to be that of collecting agency.

Thus it is even clearer here than in the *Dakin* suit

that the respondent acted as a fiduciary—that it was no more than a collecting agent. The steps taken after the receipt of the items by the respondent in this case as in that one did not change the relationship. The checks were forwarded to the drawee, were charged against the respective accounts of the drawers and a draft was forwarded to the respondent. The respondent had expressly requested return in Chicago Exchange as it was authorized to do by its contract with its customers. The draft, then, was held in an agency capacity. In fact the view of the dissenting Justice in the *Dakin* case that the acceptance of anything but cash precluded the forwarding bank from denying its ownership is inapplicable to the present situation, since the forwarding bank had an express agreement with its principals that it might take drafts as *conditional* payment. It was further agreed that "items received in payment of collections" were handled as the depositor's collecting agent. (R. 25) Notwithstanding the taking of the draft as conditional payment the Continental bank, under the agreement did not become liable to its customers until "final payment in cash or solvent credits." (R. 25) The respondent, therefore, did not step aside from its duties as agent and did not become the owner.

The fact that The McCartney National Bank had a deposit with the respondent furnishes no basis for the alleged set-off: (1) There was no showing of the existence of an agreement between respondent and the McCartney bank that respondent was to rely upon the deposit balance of the McCartney bank as security for the payment of these collection items, but on the contrary the express agreement was that remittance should be in Chicago Exchange; (2) the deposit credit was not given on the faith of the collection items. No steps were taken by the petitioner in reliance upon any supposed ownership by respondent of the forwarded items. Therefore, in spite of such deposit, if the respondent had failed, the petitioner would have had to answer to the respondent's customers, the true owners of the items. See *Wilson & Co.* v. *Smith*, 3 How. 763; *People's National Bank* v. *Payne*, 26 F. (2d) 208 (C. C. A. 8th, 1928); *Sweeney* v. *Easter*, 1 Wall. 166; *George D. Harter Bank* v. *Inglis*, 6 F. (2d) 841 (C. C. A. 6th, 1925). The case of *Bank of The Metropolis* v. *New England Bank*, 1 How. 234, 6 How. 212, distinguished by the majority in the *Dakin* case and cited by the dissenting Justice, does not hold to the contrary. In that case the two banks collected paper for each other and had mutual accounts, each having authority to deduct paper collected for the other from the balance due on the account. It was held that a lien attached on paper forwarded which was apparently owned by the forwarding bank to make good the indebtedness on this running account if credit was extended or balances allowed to remain on the faith of the paper received or to be received. In the instant case, there is no indication that the McCartney Bank placed any reliance on the paper forwarded. There is no showing of any course of dealing at all comparable to that of the banks involved in the *Metropolis* case. The McCartney Bank made no attempt to assert a lien on the items, but forwarded its draft in an attempt to make payment for them. Moreover, even if it were conceded, for the sake of argument, that if the respondent had failed the petitioner might have defeated the claims of the owners of the items by using its deposit in respondent, it by no means follows that the respondent may set off the items in the present case. The only possible basis for such a result would have been the false impression that the respondent owned the items. The owners of the items might have created such a false impression by clothing the forwarding bank with the indicia of ownership. But when the situation is reversed, the respondent cannot be allowed to say it was not collecting agent when it had expressly agreed that it was. Cf. *Beaver Boards Cos.* v. *Imbrie & Co.*, 287 F. 158 (N. D. Ga. 1923), aff'd. *Fulton National Bank* v. *Hozier*, 295 F. 611 (C. C. A. 5th, 1923); rev'd. on other grounds, 267 U. S. 276. It cannot use a deposit account it knew to be due from it as a set-off against sums it knew to be due to it only in a fiduciary capacity.

The National Bank Act (12 U. S. C. Sections 91, 192, 194) provides for the ratable distribution among creditors of the assets of insolvent banks. This Court has jealously protected the statutory provisions for such ratable distribution—even to the extent of denying the federal government preference. *Cook County Nat. Bank* v. *United States,* 107 U. S. 445; see also *Davis* v. *Elmira Savings Bank*, 161 U. S. 275. It has been repeatedly held that persons in the position of the customers of the respondent are entitled to no preference since the collection items, being drawn upon the collecting bank, did not augment the assets of The McCartney National Bank. *Larabee Flour Mills* v. *First Nat. Bank of Henryetta, Okla.*, 13 F. (2d) 330 (C. C. A. 8th, 1926), cert. denied 273 U. S. 727; *Ellerbe* v. *Studebaker Corp. of America,* 21 F. (2d) 993 (C. C. A. 4th, 1927). Similar principles have prevented the allowance of preferences where a debtor relationship is created by the acts of the parties. *Blakey* v. *Brinson*, 286 U. S. 254; *Great Atlantic & Pacific Tea Company* v. *Citizens' National Bank,* 2 Fed. Supp. 29 (W. D. Pa. 1932), aff'd. 66 F. (2d) 883 (C. C. A. 3d, 1933). This is true even though a draft has been sent to the forwarding bank. *Spurway* v. *Frick Company, Inc.*, 63 F. (2d) 875 (C. C. A. 5th, 1933); *Farmers' National Bank of Burlington, Kan.* v. *Pribble*, 15 F. (2d) 175 (C. C. A. 8th, 1926): As expressed in Stone, Legal Problems in the Transmission of Funds, 21 Col. L. Rev. 507, 525 (1921):

> "The very essence of the right of priority over other creditors depends upon the setting apart of a particular fund for the benefit of the depositor. There is no basis for giving one depositor a priority over another unless this is an essential part of the transaction."

The customers of the respondent, as the owners of the items, have claims against the petitioner and would be entitled to set off amounts they owed The McCartney National Bank, but to allow them to avail themselves of any indebtedness of their agent by way of set-off (and there might be several agents in the course of a collection) would defeat the provisions of the National Bank Act for ratable distribution. As expressly pointed out in *Krueger* v. *First National Bank of Chicago,* 217 Ill. App. 18 (1920), the purely fortuitous circumstance that the forwarding bank owes the drawee bank money should not create a right of preference otherwise illegal.

It is therefore respectfully submitted that the plaintiff is entitled to recover the deposit balance of The McCartney National Bank with the defendant, that there is no mutual debt which the defendant is entitled to set off against the amount of the deposit balance admittedly due, and that to allow the set-off claimed constitutes an illegal preference of certain creditors of the closed bank. If the set-off is denied these creditors have, as they should, their claims against the receiver. We therefore ask that the judgment of the Circuit Court of Appeals for the Seventh Circuit be reversed.

Respectfully submitted,

Amos C. Miller,
Sidney S. Gorham,
Henry W. Wales,
Edward R. Adams,
    Counsel for Petitioner.

F. G. Awalt,
George P. Barse,
John F. Anderson,
George B. Springston,
    Attorneys for Comptroller of the Currency,
        Of Counsel.

APPENDIX.

The complete agreement between the respondent and its customers, set forth in the stipulation of the parties, is:

"In receiving and handling items for deposit or collection (including items received in payment of collections) this Bank acts only as depositor's collecting agent and assumes no responsibility beyond the exercise of due care. All items are credited or cashed subject to final payment in cash or solvent credits. This Bank will not be liable for default or negligence of its correspondents, nor for losses in transit, and no correspondent shall be liable except for its own negligence. It is optional but not obligatory, to request certification in any case. This Bank or its correspondents may, as depositor's agent, send items, directly or indirectly, to any bank or to any drawee, acceptor or payor, and accept draft, check or credit as conditional payment in lieu of cash. It may charge back any item at any time before final payment, whether returned or not, also any item drawn on this Bank not good at close of business on day deposited. It may decline to honor or pay checks drawn against conditional credits. This Bank shall have a lien on all items handled by it and on the proceeds thereof for its charges, expenses (including court costs and attorney's fees) and any advances made by it in connection therewith.

"It may transmit any item for collection to any Federal Reserve Bank and such item shall be subject to the rules and regulations of such Federal Reserve Bank or of the Federal Reserve Board now in force or hereafter promulgated.

"Items payable, in the City of Chicago, or in any suburb thereof, may be collected through the Chicago Clearing House Association (in which event they may be carried over for presentation through the Clearing House on the following business day) and will be subject to its rules and regulations now in force or hereafter adopted; or they may be collected in any manner hereinbefore provided or contemplated.

"This Bank endeavors to forward items payable outside of Chicago on day of receipt, but it is understood that they need not be forwarded until the following business day." (R. 25, 26)

IN THE

Supreme Court of the United States

OCTOBER TERM, A. D. 1933.

No. 358

L. J. BOSWORTH, RECEIVER OF THE McCARTNEY NATIONAL
BANK OF GREEN BAY, WISCONSIN,

Petitioner,

vs.

CONTINENTAL ILLINOIS BANK AND TRUST
COMPANY,

Respondent.

BRIEF OF RESPONDENT.

ISAAC H. MAYER,
CARL MEYER,
DAVID F. ROSENTHAL,
FRANK D. MAYER,
Counsel for Respondent.

THE GUNTHORP-WARREN PRINTING COMPANY, 210 WEST JACKSON, CHICAGO

INDEX.

Table of Cases, Text Books and Statutes.

Statutes.

Text Books.

IN THE

Supreme Court of the United States

OCTOBER TERM, A. D. 1933.

No. 358

L. J. BOSWORTH, RECEIVER OF THE McCARTNEY NA-
TIONAL BANK OF GREEN BAY, WISCONSIN,

Petitioner,

vs.

CONTINENTAL ILLINOIS BANK AND TRUST
COMPANY,

Respondent.

BRIEF OF RESPONDENT.

SUMMARY OF ARGUMENT.

---

1. By means of the general endorsements of the
checks deposited in the defendant Continental Illinois
Bank and Trust Company the cause of action, based
upon said checks, vested in said bank and entitled it to
use the proceeds thereof as an offset against its indebtedness for the deposit balance of The McCartney National Bank with the defendant. Furthermore, the indebtedness of The McCartney National Bank to the defendant was evidenced by a remittance draft payable to
the defendant, which remained outstanding and unendorsed and upon which customers of the Continental Illinois Bank and Trust Company could not have taken action against The McCartney National Bank. The sole

right of action upon such draft was in the defendant, Continental Illinois Bank and Trust Company. 2. In every reported case in which the dishonored remittance draft has been charged against the collecting bank's deposit with the forwarding bank, the offset has been allowed. 3. The facts in *Dakin* v. *Bayly*, 78 L. Ed. 95 (No. 44, October term, decided November 20, 1933), are different in several respects from those in the case at bar, and the cases relied upon by the court in deciding that case are distinguishable.* 4. The sole question involved is the right of offset. Where a setoff is otherwise valid its allowance does not constitute a preference.

---

* It is true that this case, as did the Dakin case, involves the rights of set-off as between a collecting and forwarding bank in case of the insolvency of the former. The facts in this case differ, however, in respects hereinafter pointed out, from those in the case of *Dakin* v. *Bayly* and we feel it our duty to fully argue the matter so that this Court may not leave open to doubt the scope of the Dakin decision.

ARGUMENT.

I.

THE CAUSE OF ACTION BASED UPON THE CHECKS FORWARDED FOR COLLECTION BY THE CONTINENTAL ILLINOIS BANK AND TRUST COMPANY TO THE MC CARTNEY NATIONAL BANK AND THE REMITTANCE DRAFT, VESTED IN THE CONTINENTAL ILLINOIS BANK AND TRUST COMPANY. IT THEREFORE HAD A RIGHT TO OFFSET SUCH CAUSE OF ACTION AGAINST ITS INDEBTEDNESS TO THE MC CARTNEY NATIONAL BANK FOR THE DEPOSIT BALANCE.

The checks which were deposited for collection in the defendant, Continental Illinois Bank and Trust Company and which were by it forwarded to The McCartney Bank for collection had been endorsed by the customers of the defendant, "Pay to the order of Continental Illinois Bank and Trust Company" or "Pay to any bank or banker. (R. 29.) The first endorsement was such as to unqualifiedly vest the title in the Continental Illinois Bank and Trust Company. The weight of authority is that the second endorsement also is nonrestrictive. (See Brannan on Negotiable Instruments, 5th Ed., p. 433.) Assuming for the sake of argument, however, that the second form of endorsement is restrictive, nevertheless, under such an endorsement the endorsee has the right "to bring any action thereon that the endorser could bring." (Sec. 37 of the Uniform Negotiable Instruments Law; Chapter 98, Sec. 57, Cahill's Illinois Revised Statutes, 1933.) It follows from the fact that the defendant had a cause of action against The McCartney National Bank, that it could offset such cause of action against the latter's claim against the defendant for the deposit balance.

In addition to the endorsement of the checks, defend-was the payee of the draft drawn by The McCartney National Bank in remittance of the proceeds and checks sent for collection. (R. 23.) Defendant was not only the payee but was the holder of the draft which was un-endorsed and as such, under Section 51 of the Uniform Negotiable Instruments Law (Chapter 98, Sec. 51, Cahill's Illinois Revised Statutes, 1933), had the right to sue thereon in its own name, and payment to it in due course would discharge the obligation of The McCartney National Bank. (See Brannan's Negotiable Instruments Laws, 5th Ed. p. 479.)

So long as the draft remained unendorsed and in the possession of the Continental Illinois Bank and Trust Company no other person could bring any action there-on nor could the McCartney Bank safely pay the amount thereof to defendant's customers or to any other person in order to discharge its liability.

In *Fuller, et al. v. Hooper*, 3 Gray 334, the Supreme Court of Massachusetts said (p. 341):

"When an agent signs an instrument, without disclosing his agency on its face, the holder must look to him alone, and *when such an instrument, which is intended for the benefit of the principal, is given to the agent only, he only, or his endorsee, can sue on it.*" (Italics ours.)

In *Brewster v. Seeger*, 173 Mass. 281, Mr. Justice Holmes said in his opinion, at p. 283:

"It is familiar law that one who is not named or described as party to a negotiable instrument, cannot sue upon it."

From the foregoing authorities and upon reason it is clear that all rights of action upon the collection items

and the remittance draft were in the Continental Illinois
Bank and Trust Company, and not its customers, and
that the defendant is therefore entitled to the offset.

II.

IN EVERY REPORTED CASE IN WHICH THE DISHONORED REMIT-
TANCE DRAFT HAS BEEN CHARGED AGAINST THE COLLECT-
ING BANK'S DEPOSIT WITH THE FORWARDING BANK, THE
OFFSET HAS BEEN ALLOWED.

In *Storing* v. *First National Bank of Minneapolis*, 28
Fed. (2nd) 587, and *Nomland, Receiver of the National
State Bank of Stockton, Kansas* v. *The First National
Bank of Kansas City*, 64 Fed. (2nd) 399, the Circuit
Courts of Appeals for the 5th and the 8th Circuit
respectively, just as the trial court and the Court of Appeals in this case, have held that a bank forwarding items
for collection had the right to apply, as an offset against
its indebtedness on account of the deposit of the collecting bank, the amount of such collection items.

In *Keyes, as Receiver of the First National Bank of
Clarkfield, Minnesota* v. *Federal Reserve Bank of Min-
neapolis*, an unreported decision of the United States
District Court of Minnesota, a case in which the ma-
terial facts were identical with those in the case at bar,
District Judge Page Morris held:

"It seems to me that defendant then had a right
of action against that bank for said amount in its
own name and in its own right. And if this is true,
it is clear it has had that right ever since, and therefore has the right of set-off. The receiver, the
plaintiff here, took the assets of the bank as a mere
trustee for creditors, and not for value and without
notice, and, in the absence of statute to the contrary,
subject to all claims and defenses that might have
been interposed as against the insolvent bank. The
subsequent charging back of the checks by defendant

* * * would not in any way affect the conclusion. The recovery of the set-off here will fully protect the plaintiff and he has no interest in, and is not concerned to inquire into, what was done between defendant and the banks depositing these checks * * *."

In *Farmers Deposit National Bank* v. *Penn Bank*, 123 Pa. State, 283; 16 Atl. 761), a cashier's check of the Penn Bank belonging to the Germania Savings Bank was deposited by the Germania Savings Bank with the Farmers Deposit National Bank. Said check was deposited May 24, 1883, and credit given by the Farmers Bank to the Germania Savings Bank for its amount. May 24th was a Saturday, and on Monday, the 26th, the Penn Bank, the drawer of the cashier's check, closed its doors. Thereupon the Farmers Bank notified the Germania Savings Bank of this and charged its account with the amount of the said check, which had been received with the right expressly reserved to charge it back. The Penn Bank had a deposit balance of $23,218.59 with the Farmers Deposit National Bank. The latter insisted on the right to use the deposit as an offset against the cashier's check which had been deposited with it as aforesaid. The receiver of the Penn Bank, who was in identically the same position as the receiver of The McCartney National Bank, claimed that the Farmers Bank had no such right of offset, and sued to recover the amount of the deposit. The trial court denied the right of offset, and entered judgment for plaintiff. In reversing this judgment the Supreme Court of Pennsylvania held, at page 291:

"In a suit brought by the assignee of the Penn Bank against the said Farmers Deposit Bank to recover a balance of $23,218.59, admittedly due the Penn Bank at the time of its failure, the Farmers Deposit Bank attempted to use the check of $88,000 as a set-off. The court below instructed the jury that the latter bank could not so use it. This is the one error of the case and it runs all through it.

The theory of this ruling was that the check belonged to the Germania Savings Bank, and a large amount of time was wasted in trying this unimportant fact. *Of what possible concern was it to the Penn Bank whether the defendant held it for collection or for value? It had no defense to the check in the hands of either bank.* If there had been a defense as to the Germania then the Penn Bank might have called upon the defendant to show that it had paid value. But as the case stood—with no defense as to either bank—it had no standing to inquire into the relations between the defendant and the Germania, any more than if the check had been presented at its counter and payment demanded before its insolvency.

If we concede that the defendant was a mere collecting bank, so far as this check was concerned, it does not alter the case. As such its title was sufficient to maintain a suit in its own name. This is settled law: *Brown v. Clark,* 14 Pa. 469; *Ward v. Tyler,* 52 Pa. 393. *If it could maintain a suit on this check in its own name, it is difficult to see any good reason why it could not set the check off in a suit against it by the assignee of the Penn Bank.* The rights of the assignee rise no higher than those of his assignor. Neither the Penn Bank nor its assignee has any concern with the question of the ownership of the check, unless a defense be shown as against the Germania, or that the defendant became the holder after the assignment. As no defense was set up against the check in the hands of anyone, and as it is an undisputed fact that the defendant became the lawful holder thereof several days before the assignment, we are all of opinion that the set-off should have been allowed." (Italics ours.)

In *Midland National Bank and Trust Company of Minneapolis* v. *First State Bank of Sioux Falls,* 175 Minn. 555, 222 N. W. 274, the Midland National Bank and Trust Company of Minneapolis forwarded checks

to the First State Bank of Sioux Falls for collection
and remittance. The items were drawn on various
banks in Sioux Falls, and collected by the First State
Bank which forwarded remittance drafts to the plaintiff. These drafts were unpaid because of the failure
of the First State Bank. The latter had deposited with
plaintiff bank certain collateral to secure any loan or
indebtedness of the First State Bank to the Midland National, and it was to foreclose the said collateral on the
basis of the indebtedness evidenced by said remittance
drafts that plaintiff filed suit. The defense asserted was
that plaintiff, having charged back the credits to its customers, and the latter being the real owners of the remittance drafts, could not apply the collateral to such indebtedness. The Supreme Court, in affirming judgment
for plaintiff and holding that the collateral was applicable to the remittance drafts, held, at page 275:

> "Immediately upon the failure of the Sioux Falls
> bank to pay, the plaintiff had a cause of action
> against it for the amount which it had collected and
> did not pay. It had the legal title, so to speak, to
> the dishonored drafts drawn by the Sioux Falls
> bank. Whatever right it had arose upon the failure
> of the bank to remit what it received, and its right
> was protected by the security of the pledge agree-
> ment. * * * It was right that the collateral held
> under the pledge agreement should respond to the
> payment of the moneys collected. The charging off
> of the credits was a matter between the plaintiff
> bank and its customers. Neither the South Dakota
> bank nor its creditors nor those representing them
> in this action should gain by it."

III.

THE FACTS IN DAKIN V. BAYLY, 78 L. ED. 95 (NO. 44, OCTOBER TERM, DECIDED NOVEMBER 20, 1933.) ARE DIFFERENT IN SEVERAL RESPECTS FROM THOSE IN THE CASE AT BAR.

In the Dakin case, the forwarding bank was not attempting (as is the case here) to charge the amount of the checks which it forwarded against funds which belonged to the insolvent bank but was attempting to charge such amount against funds which belonged to or were impressed with a trust in favor of the insolvent bank's customers. Indeed, this court in the Dakin case specifically pointed out that the insolvent bank carried no deposit with the forwarding bank.

In the Dakin case the defendant bank, in so far as the record shows, had given no credit to its customers upon the deposit of the checks in question. In our case the defendant's customers were credited with the amount of the checks upon their deposit. (R. 23.) It is true that such credit was subject to a charge back at any time before final payment and might decline to honor or to pay checks drawn against conditional credits, but, nevertheless, the credits remained on the books of the defendant. No charge backs were made until after insolvency. Inasmuch as the rights of the parties are fixed as of the date of insolvency (*Scott* v. *Armstrong*, 146 U. S. 499, and cases heretofore cited in this brief), such charges to its customers by the defendant are wholly immaterial.

In the *Dakin* case the rights of the parties and the alleged agency relationship between the defendant bank and its customers were established by the Florida statutes. In our case the alleged agency relationship is established by private contract between the Continental Bank and its customers, and there was nothing to place the collecting bank or the plaintiff receiver on notice of the contract between the Continental and its customers. The rights as between the Continental and the closed bank (and the receiver) are therefore to be governed by the relationship established by the endorsements on the checks. In so far as the endorsements showed, this defendant was not an agent but was the real party in interest. As held in the decisions which we have heretofore cited, the relationship between the defendant and its customers was of no concern to the receiver of The McCartney National Bank.

In the *Dakin* case in support of the proposition that "a defendant sued upon his individual debt may not avail himself for this purpose of a demand against the plaintiff held in a fiduciary capacity, the court cited the cases of *Central National Bank of Baltimore* v. *Connecticut Mutual Life Insurance Co.*, 104 U. S. 54; *Libby* v. *Hopkins*, 104 U. S. 303; *Western Tie & Timber Co.* v. *Brown*, 196 U. S. 502; *United States* v. *Butterworth-Judson Corporation*, 267 U. S. 387, 394-5; *Thomas* v. *Potter Title and Trust Company*, 2 Fed. Supp. 12.

In the first of these cases, this court merely held that the bank's right of offset "cannot be permitted to prevail against the equity of the beneficial owner, of which the bank has notice, either actual or constructive." In the case at bar there were no intervening equities and the defendant here is not attempting to appropriate a *trust* fund to payment of its individual claim. It is merely attempting to apply to the payment of a draft to which it holds title, funds belonging to the insolvent bank in its individual capacity. It may well be held that if in the Dakin case the St. Petersburg bank had never closed, and had sued on the checks which it had forwarded to the Clearwater bank, for collection for the account of its *customers*, the Clearwater bank could not have set off the amount of its customer's checks which it had sent to the St. Petersburg bank for collector and for which the latter had remitted by a draft payable to the order of the St. Petersburg bank and thereafter dishonored. It does not follow from such a holding that, had the St. Petersburg bank had a deposit account with the Clearwater bank, the dishonored draft to which the Clearwater bank had title could not be charged against such deposit account. Such is the present case and the rights of the receiver of the McCartney National Bank can be and are no greater than were the rights of that bank. (*Scott* v. *Armstrong,* 146 U. S. 499, 507.)

In *Libby* v. *Hopkins,* 104 U. S. 303, *Western Tie & Timber Co.* v. *Brown,* 196 U. S. 502, and *United States* v. *Butterworth-Jutson Corporation,* 367 U. S. 387, other cases cited by this court in the Dakin opinion, the court refused to allow offsets against funds which had been deposited under specific instructions on the theory that to allow the offset would in each instance have deprived beneficiaries of a trust of rights to which they were entitled. *Thomas* v. *Potter Title & Trust Co., supra,* is a case where defendant as trustee had a deposit with plaintiff. Since plaintiff had knowledge of the trust, defendant was not allowed to use as an offset plaintiff's deposit with defendant. The cases are, therefore, in no way pertinent or applicable to the facts of the case at bar.

IV.

THE SOLE QUESTION INVOLVED IS THE RIGHT OF OFFSET, AND
IF THE OFFSET IS PROPER THERE CAN BE NO PREFERENCE.

By arguing that the offset, if allowed, would constitute
an illegal preference petitioner begs the question. If the
set-off is properly allowed, then there is no preference.
As said by this court in *Scott* v. *Armstrong,* 146 U. S.
499, at page 510:

"Where a set-off is otherwise valid, it is not perceived how its allowance can be considered a preference, and it is clear that it is only the balance, if
any, after the set-off is deducted which can justly be
held to form part of the assets of the insolvent. The
requirement as to ratable dividends, is to make them
from what belongs to the Bank, and that which at
the time of the insolvency belongs of right to the
debtor does not belong to the Bank."

For the foregoing reasons we respectfully submit that
the judgment of the Circuit Court of Appeals for the
Seventh Circuit be affirmed.

Respectfully submitted,
ISAAC H. MAYER,
CARL MEYER,
DAVID F. ROSENTHAL,
FRANK D. MAYER,
Counsel for Respondent.

APPENDIX.

OPINION OF THE DISTRICT COURT OF MINNESOTA IN THE UNREPORTED CASE OF KEYES, AS RECEIVER OF FIRST NATIONAL BANK OF CLARKFIELD, MINNESOTA v. FEDERAL RESERVE BANK OF MINNEAPOLIS.

MEMORANDUM.

At all times mentioned herein the First National Bank of Clarkfield, Minnesota, was a national banking association duly incorporated under the pursuant to the banking laws of the United States, and up to the 18th of September, 1917, conducted business as a national bank at Clarkfield, Minnesota.

At all times mentioned herein the defendant was a corporation duly organized and existing under and pursuant to an act of Congress of the United States entitled "Federal Reserve Act," approved December 23d, 1913, and conducting the business of a Federal Reserve Bank at Minneapolis, Minnesota.

The plaintiff's insolvent, First National Bank of Clarkfield, Minnesota, was on the 18th day of September, 1917, insolvent, and was on that day closed by order of the Comptroller of the Currency under and by virtue of the power and authority conferred upon him by the banking laws of the United States, and by virtue of the same power and authority the plaintiff was appointed as receiver thereof and on the 4th day of October, 1917, duly qualified as such receiver. Said First National Bank of Clarkfield was a member bank of the defendant under the provisions of the Federal Reserve Act. Pursuant to the provisions of the Federal Reserve Act the Federal Reserve Board, in the month of June, 1916, established a collection and clearing system by rules and regulations which have since been in force and effect, and prior to the transactions herein involved the defendant had become a part of such collection and clearing system, under such rules and regulations. The rules and regulations of the Federal Reserve Board provide, under the heading "Check Clearing and Collecting," as follows:

(Exhibit "C"):

Each Federal Reserve Bank shall exercise the functions of a clearing house under the following general terms and conditions:

(1) Each Federal Reserve Bank will receive at par from its member banks and from non-member banks in its district which have become clearing members checks drawn on all member and clearing member banks and on all other non-member banks which agree to remit at par through the Federal Reserve Bank of their district.

(2) Each Federal reserve bank will receive at par from other Federal Reserve Banks and will receive at par from all member and clearing member banks, regardless of their location, for the credit of their accounts with their respective Federal Reserve Banks, checks drawn upon all member and clearing member banks of its district and upon all other non-member banks of its district whose checks can be collected at par by the Federal Reserve Bank. The Federal Reserve Banks will prepare a par list of all nonmember banks to be revised from time to time, which will be furnished to member and clearing member banks.

(3) Immediate credit entry upon receipt subject to final payment will be made for all such items upon the books of the Federal Reserve Bank at full face value but the proceeds will not be counted as part of the minimum reserve nor become available to meet checks drawn until actually collected, in accordance with the best practice now prevailing.

(4) Checks received by a Federal Reserve Bank on its member or clearing member banks will be forwarded direct to such banks and will not be charged to their accounts until sufficient time has elapsed within which to receive advise of payment.

(5) In the selection of collecting agents for handling checks on nonmember banks, which have not become clearing members, member banks will be given the preference.

(6) Under this plan each Federal Reserve Bank will receive at par from its member and clearing member banks checks on all member and clearing member banks and on all other nonmember banks whose checks can be

collected at par by any Federal Reserve Bank. Member
and clearing member banks will be required by the Federal Reserve Board to provide funds to cover at par all
checks received from or for the account of their Federal
Reserve Banks. Provided, however, that a member or
clearing member bank may ship currency or specie from
its own vaults at the expense of its Federal Reserve
Bank to cover any deficiency which may arise because of
and only in the case of inability to provide items to offset checks received from or for the account of its Federal Reserve Bank.

(7) Section 19 of the Federal Reserve Act provides
that—

The required balance carried by a member bank with
a Federal Reserve Bank may, under the regulations and
subject to such penalties as may be prescribed by the
Federal Reserve Board, be checked against and withdrawn by such member bank for the purpose of meeting
existing liabilities: Provided, however, that no bank
shall at any time make new loans or shall pay any dividends unless and until the total balance required by law
is fully restored.

It is manifest that items in process of collection can
not lawfully be counted as part of the minimum reserve
balance to be carried by a member bank with its Federal
Reserve Bank. Therefore, should a member bank draw
against such items the draft would be charged against its
reserve balance if such balance were sufficient in amount
to pay it; but any resulting impairment of reserve balances would be subject to all the penalties provided by
the Act.

Inasmuch as it is essential that the law in respect to
the maintenance by member banks of the required minimum reserve balance shall be strictly complied with, the
Federal Reserve Board, under authority vested in it by
section 19 of the Act, hereby prescribes as the penalty
for any deficiency in reserves a sum equivalent to an
interest charge on the amount of the deficiency of 2 per
cent. per annum above the ninety day discount rate of
the Federal Reserve Bank of the district in which the
member bank is located. The Board reserves the right
to increase this penalty whenever conditions require it.

For the purpose of keeping their reserve balances intact member banks may at all times have recourse to the rediscount facilities offered by their respective Federal Reserve Banks.

(8) Each Federal Reserve Bank will determine by analysis the amounts of uncollected funds appearing on its books to the credit of each member bank. Such analysis will show the true status of the reserve held by the Federal Reserve Bank for each member bank and will enable it to apply the penalty for impairment of reserve.

A schedule of the time required within which to collect checks will be furnished to each bank to enable it to determine the time at which any item sent to its Federal Reserve Bank will be counted as reserve and become available to meet any checks drawn.

(9) In handling items for member and clearing member banks, a Federal Reserve Bank will act as agent only. The Board will require that each member and clearing member bank authorize its Federal Reserve Bank to send checks for collection to banks on which checks are drawn, and, except for negligence, such Federal Reserve Bank will assume no liability. Any further requirements that the Board may deem necessary will be set forth by the Federal Reserve Banks in their letters of instruction to their member and clearing member banks. Each Federal Reserve Bank will also promulgate rules and regulations governing the details of its operations as a clearing house such rules and regulations to be binding upon all member and non-member banks which are clearing through the Federal Reserve Bank.

And the rules and regulations governing the details of its operations as a clearing house promulgated by defendant provide, under the heading "Check Clearing and Collecting," as follows (Exhibit "B"):

1. The Federal Reserve Bank of Minneapolis will discontinue its present collection system on July 15, 1916, in accordance with Federal Reserve Board Circular 1, Series of 1916, already sent you, and will thereafter, until further notice, receive from its member banks for immediate credit at par, checks drawn on all member banks in the United States and on such non-member banks as can be collected at par.

A par list of all non-member banks will be prepared,

to be revised from time to time, which will be furnished member banks.

All such checks, except those drawn on Minneapolis and St. Paul banks, received by the Federal Reserve Bank by 3:00 P. M., except Saturday, when the hour will be 12:00 o'clock noon, will be credited subject to final payment at full face value upon day of receipt. Those received later than these hours will be credited upon the following business day. *The proceeds, however, will not be counted as reserve, nor become available, to meet checks drawn, until actually collected.* Owing to the clearing hour, checks drawn on Minneapolis and St. Paul banks received after 10:30 A. M., will not be credited nor proceeds become available until the following business day; those received before that hour will be credited on day of receipt and proceeds will be available that day.

3. Checks received by the Federal Reserve Bank, drawn on its member banks, will be forwarded direct to such member banks, and *will be charged to their accounts on the date which, under usual conditions, advice of payment may be expected.* Member banks should *credit* all remittances received from the Federal Reserve Bank upon day of receipt, advising the Federal Reserve Bank, and should not remit their drafts in payment. *Member banks are required by the Federal Reserve Board to provide funds to cover at par all checks received from, or for the account of, their Federal Reserve Bank.*

Section 19 of the Federal Reserve Act provides that:

"The reserve carried by a member bank with a Federal Reserve Bank may, under the regulations, subject to such penalties as may be prescribed by the Federal Reserve Board, be checked against and withdrawn by such member bank for the purpose of meeting existing liabilities; Provided, however, *that no bank shall at any time make new loans or shall pay any dividends unless and until the total reserve required by law is fully restored.*"

7. In handling items for member banks, the Federal Reserve Bank of Minneapolis acts as agent only. It is understood that each member bank authorizes it to send checks for collection direct to banks on which checks are drawn, and except for negligence the Federal Reserve

Bank of Minneapolis assumes no liability until funds are actually in its hands.

In September, 1917, there was and still is at Clarkfield, Minnesota, where the First National Bank of Clarkfield was located and doing business, a bank organized under the laws of Minnesota called the Clarkfield State Bank; and during all of said month this bank was a non-member bank of defendant upon which defendant could collect checks at par; and said bank was on the par list of non-member banks prepared by defendant and furnished to its member banks in accordance with said rules and regulations.

On the 17th of September, 1917, checks payable on presentation amounting to $1998.21 were deposited with defendant. These checks to the amount of $1943.96 were on said Clarkfield State Bank and to the amount of $54.25 on said First National Bank of Clarkfield. These checks to the amount of $548.49 were so deposited by the Northwestern National Bank, Minneapolis, Minnesota, a member bank of defendant; and to the amount of $555.21 by the Merchants National Bank of St. Paul, Minnesota, a member bank of defendant; and to the amount of $218.30 by the Peoples Bank of St. Paul, Minnesota, a member bank of defendant; and one check for $570.86 by the First National Bank of Chicago, Illinois, a national banking association, and as such a member of the Federal Reserve Bank; and one check for $5.35 by the Corn Exchange National Bank of Chicago, Illinois, a national banking association, and as such a member of the Federal Reserve Bank; and one check for $100. by the Des Moines National Bank of Des Moines, Iowa, a national banking association, and as such a member of the Federal Reserve Bank. Each check when deposited with defendant contained on the back thereof the unrestricted and unconditional endorsements in blank of the payee thereof and of the bank depositing the same with defendant and credit was on that day given by defendant at par to the bank depositing the same.

After said checks were deposited with defendant and credit given for them as aforesaid, and on said 17th day of September, 1917, defendant forwarded all said checks by mail to said First National Bank of Clarkfield, for payment and credit as to the checks for $54.25 on said bank, and for collection and credit as to the checks for $1943.96 on the Clarkfield State Bank, and all said checks were received by said First National Bank of Clarkfield on the 18th day of September, 1917.

On said 18th of September, 1917, the First National Bank of Clarkfield cleared with said Clarkfield State Bank checks which each then held against the other, and in this clearing the First National Bank of Clarkfield used all the checks on the State Bank of Clarkfield received from defendant as aforesaid and received credit for the same from said Clarkfield State Bank, but received no money. In said clearing the First National Bank of Clarkfield surrendered and delivered to the Clarkfield State Bank as fully paid and cancelled, all the checks on the latter bank which it had received from defendant, and the First National Bank of Clarkfield thereupon and on said 18th of September, 1917, and before it was closed or a receiver appointed for it, gave defendant credit on its books for all the checks which it received from defendant on that day as aforesaid, to-wit: for the sum of $1998.21.

The checks for $54.25 on the First National Bank of Clarkfield were returned by said bank or the plaintiff to the various drawers thereof, and the checks for $1943.96 on the Clarkfield State Bank were returned by it to the various drawers thereof, by reason whereof a more particular description of any of said checks can not be given.

No remittance or payment was ever made to defendant or any of the payees or endorsers of any of the above mentioned checks for or on account of such checks, or for or on account of the credit which defendant received on the books of said First National Bank of Clarkfield for said checks.

Thereafter, and on the 16th of October, 1917, defendant charged back severally to the various banks which had deposited the checks aforesaid, amounting to $1998.21, the amount of said checks which had been so deposited by each of said banks. And thereafter, and on the 14th day of May, 1918, this action was brought.

On the 18th of September, 1917, the First National Bank of Clarkfield had a balance to its credit on the books of defendant of $8647.04. On the 25th of January, 1918, upon an accounting between plaintiff and defendant it was found that said bank was entitled to a credit for the amount of its stock in defendant with dividends accrued thereon to September 1, 1917, of $963., and to a further credit for unearned discounts on notes due March 1, 1918, of $21.90, making in all $9631.94, and that defendant had a right to deduct therefrom the amount of certain forged notes (the forgery having been discovered after the closing of the bank for insolvency), with interest which had been discounted by said bank with defendant prior to the 18th of September, 1917, for the purpose of replenishing the reserve of said bank with defendant and the proceeds of which forged notes constituted a part of said balance of $8647.04. After making these credits and deductions a balance of $1536.15 was found to be due from defendant to said bank unless defendant has the right to set off against this balance the amount of the aforesaid checks for $1998.21.

On said 18th of September, 1917, and for some time prior thereto, said First National Bank of Clarkfield was insolvent and was known by its cashier and one of its directors to be insolvent.

The sole contention and question to be decided here is as to whether or not the defendant is entitled to offset against the aforesaid balance of $1536.15 the amount of the aforesaid checks $1998.21, the plaintiff contending that it has not the right to do so and the defendant that it has.

Under the pleadings and proofs here whether the offset be legal or equitable in its nature the right to its allowance can be determined in this action U. S. Comp. Statutes, Sec. 1251-b (Judicial Code 247-b, as amended by Act of March, 1915, Ch. 90, 38 U. S. Statutes at large, 956.)

That defendant handled said checks as a clearing house, for the purpose of collection and clearing, and for no other purpose, is mutually conceded by counsel. Considering the matter then as a clearing house transaction it seems to me clear that, if the First National Bank of Clarkfield and the Clarkfield State Bank had been banks doing business in Minneapolis and the clearing had been had there on the 18th of September, 1917, upon finding that the $1998.21 was due from the First National

Bank of Clarkfield to defendant, the defendant would
have had the right to immediate payment thereof to it
by that bank either in money or by check on its balance
with defendant, or to charge said amount to said bank's
account and have said bank give it credit therefor, and
that being done the transaction would have been com-
pletely closed. But the defendant was the clearing house
for banks in a wide territory, embracing the whole state
of Minnesota, and was the clearing house for these two
Clarkfield banks, and these checks had to be forwarded
by mail and the clearance had at Clarkfield. It is not apparent that upon the clearance being had between the
Clarkfield banks defendant had the right to a credit with
the First National Bank of Clarkfield for this amount
and to charge the same to the account of said bank?
That credit was given, but the charge was not made. It
seems to me that defendant then had a right of action
against that bank for said amount in its own name and
in its own right. And if this is true, it is clear it has
had that right ever since, and therefore has the right of
set off. The receiver, the plaintiff here, took the assets
of the bank as a mere trustee for creditors, and not for
value and without notice, and, in the absence of statute
to the contrary, subject to all claims and defenses that
might have been interposed as against the insolvent bank.
The subsequent charging back of the checks by defendant or the subsequent statements of counsel for the defendant in his letters would not in any way affect the
conclusion. The recovery of the set off here will fully
protect the plaintiff and he has no interest in, and is not
concerned to inquire into, what was done between defendant and the banks depositing these checks or what
advice has been given to defendant by its counsel, *Elmquist* v. *Markot*, 45 Minn. 305, *Vanstrum* v. *Liljengren*,
37 Minn. 191.

But let us consider the matter not as a clearing house
transaction but as one of any agency for collection. The
whole argument of plaintiff's counsel rests upon the
proposition that as at the time the suit was brought the
defendant was not the owner of the checks, they having,
on the 16th of October, 1917, been charged back to the
banks which had deposited them with defendant for collection, defendant has now no right of set off. He also
quotes from letters written by defendant's counsel sub-

sequent to the closing of the bank which he contends support his proposition, and he claims that these letters and the charging back of the checks work an estoppel against the defendant's now asserting the right of set off. It does not seem to me that these statements of counsel and the charging back of the checks in any way affect the rights of the parties here. As to the claim of estoppel it may be said that the most essential element of an estoppel is absent. In the charging back of the checks and the statements of counsel for defendant there has been no act, representation or concealment upon which plaintiff or his insolvent has been induced to act, nor has there been any action by plaintiff or his inoslvent in reliance thereon of a character to result in substantial prejudice to him or to his insolvent or to the creditors for whom as receiver he is trustee of the assets of the insolvent. It seems to me that the rights of the parties became fixed as of the time of the closing of the bank. *Scott* v. *Armstrong*, 146 U. S. 499-511. At that time defendant had a right of action against plaintiff's insolvent for the amount of the checks, whether or not they were only received by it as an agent for collection and conditional credit, and whether or not the endorsements thereon were restricted or unrestricted. General statutes of Minnesota 1913, Section 5848 and 5849. The subsequent ownership of the checks is unimportant. There was no defense as to the checks and no defense as to the credit arising therefrom on the books of the insolvent bank. The plaintiff has no standing to inquire into the relations between defendant and its depositing banks. Neither the insolvent nor its receiver has any concern with the question of the ownership of the checks, unless a defense be shown as against the endorsers or drawers thereof, or that defendant became the holder thereof after the closing of the bank for insolvency, or after knowledge of its insolvency. There is no such showing, and on the contrary the opposite appears. *Farmers Deposit National Bank* v. *Penn. Bank*, 123 Pa. 283, *Penn. Bank* v. *Farmers Deposit National Bank*, 130 Pa. 209.

Plaintiff's counsel contends that the allowance of the offset would work a preference contrary to the provisions of Sections 5234, 5236 and 5242, Revised Statutes of the U. S. 1878 (the National Banking Act). This contention is, I think, fully disposed of adversely thereto by the decision of the Supreme Court in the case of *Scott* v. *Armstrong, supra.*

I am therefore of the opinion that defendant is legally entitled to the set off in question. And if I am in error as to that, I still think that under all the facts and circumstances of this case it is equitably entitled hereto. *Scott* v. *Armstrong, supra.* It must be remembered that the insolvent bank and its creditors received the full benefit of the amount of the checks. If the doctrine of estoppel can be invoked at all here, it would be to prevent the receiver from objecting to the setoff; at least to the amount of $1943.96, the amount of the checks drawn on the State Bank of Clarkfield. Plaintiff's insolvent was, on the 18th of September, 1917, and for some time prior thereto, insolvent, and known to be so by its chief managing officer. Notwithstanding that fact it held itself out to be solvent, and received and handled these checks as above set forth. Relying on its solvency and induced by its holding itself out to be so, defendant forwarded these checks to it when it might have forwarded them direct to the State Bank of Clarkfield, which of course was to the substantial prejudice of defendant.

The result is, that the balance of $1536.15 is wiped out; and defendant has the right to a claim against the receiver for the difference between that amount and $1998.21, the amount of the checks, to-wit, $462.06.

PAGE MORRIS

Judge.

IN THE

Supreme Court of the United States

OCTOBER TERM, A. D. 1933.

———

No. 358.

———

L. J. BOSWORTH, Receiver of The McCartney National Bank of Green Bay, Wisconsin, *Petitioner,*

vs.

CONTINENTAL ILLINOIS BANK AND TRUST COMPANY, *Respondent.*

———

REPLY BRIEF OF PETITIONER.

———

AMOS C. MILLER,
SIDNEY S. GORHAM,
HENRY W. WALES,
EDWARD R. ADAMS,
  Counsel for Petitioner.

F. G. AWALT,
GEORGE P. BARSE,
JOHN F. ANDERSON,
GEORGE B. SPRINGSTON,
  Attorneys for Comptroller
  of the Currency,
    Of Counsel.

PRESS OF BYRON S. ADAMS, WASHINGTON, D. C.

INDEX.

CASES CITED.

IN THE

Supreme Court of the United States

OCTOBER TERM, A. D. 1933.

No. 358.

L. J. Bosworth, Receiver of The McCartney National Bank of Green Bay, Wisconsin, *Petitioner,*

vs.

Continental Illinois Bank and Trust Company, *Respondent.*

REPLY BRIEF OF PETITIONER.

A. REPLY TO POINTS I AND II OF RESPONDENT.

Point I of Respondent, that Respondent had a cause of action against the McCartney Bank upon the checks forwarded for collection to the latter, and upon the draft drawn by the McCartney Bank in remittance of the proceeds of said checks, and that therefore such causes of action could be offset against the deposit of the McCartney Bank, is effectively answered by the recent decision of this Court of Dakin v. Bayly, 290 U. S. 143, (No. 44, decided November 20, 1933) which has been discussed in Petitioner's main brief.

Respondent's second point, that in every reported case in which a dishonored remittance draft has been charged against the collecting bank's deposit with the forwarding bank, the offset has been allowed, is likewise answered by the Dakin v. Bayly decision.

B. IN POINT III OF RESPONDENT'S BRIEF AT-TEMPT IS MADE TO DIFFERENTIATE THE INSTANT CASE FROM THE DAKIN V. BAYLY CASE FROM THE STANDPOINT OF THE FACTS INVOLVED.

Respondent first states that in the Dakin case the for-warding bank was attempting to charge the amount of the collection items against items which it held impressed with a trust in favor of the insolvent bank's customers, and that in the instant case the forwarding bank is attempting to charge the offset against a deposit belonging to the insol-vent bank. The fact is that the Dakin case was not decided on the supposition that the funds held by the forwarding bank were impressed with a trust in favor of the insolvent bank's customers on the theory of agency of the insolvent bank for its customers, but was decided on the supposition that the funds held by the forwarding bank (the Clear-water Bank) belong to the insolvent bank (the St. Peters-burg Bank). Hence in that respect the two cases are iden-tical in principle in that in each case the funds held by the forwarding bank belonged to the insolvent or collecting bank in its own right and of course it would be immaterial in this respect whether said funds represented a deposit belonging to the collecting bank or proceeds of other items belonging to the insolvent bank.

Respondent next states that in the Dakin case, insofar as the record shows, no credit was given by the forward-ing bank to its customers covering the checks there in ques-tion, whereas in the instant case the forwarding bank did credit its depositors with the amounts of the forwarded checks. This point was discussed on page 7 of Petitioner's main brief and as there pointed out such provisional cred-its did not render the forwarding bank the owner of a claim against the insolvent or collecting bank (St. Louis and San Francisco Railway Company v. Johnston, 133 U. S. 566). However, the whole matter in this respect is answered by the fact that the contract between the forwarding bank and its depositors in the instant case clearly provided that the forwarding bank was to continue to be agent for its depositors until final payment for the checks had been received. The act of the forwarding bank in charging the items back recognized the continued agency.

Respondent next states that in the Dakin case the agency relationship between the forwarding bank and its depositors was established by statute, whereas the agency relationship in the instant case was established by private contract between the Continental Bank and its customers, "and there was nothing to place the collecting bank *or the plaintiff receiver* on notice of the contract between the Continental and its customers". Respondent then argues that as a consequence the rights between the Continental Bank and the McCartney Bank were to be governed by the relationship established by the endorsements on the checks.

Regardless of the notice or lack of notice which the McCartney Bank may have had as to the relation between the Continental Bank and its depositors, the fact is, (and this suit is based upon such fact), that the receiver had notice that the Continental Bank was only an agent for its customers, and that the real ownership of the funds owed by the McCartney Bank for the collected items was and is in the depositors of the Continental Bank, as result of which the depositors had the right, and still have the right, to file claims against the McCartney Bank for the amounts of such items, and also have the right to offset such claims against any claims which the McCartney Bank may have against them. It is of course thoroughly established doctrine that when a bank is put upon notice of ownership of funds claimed by third parties adversely to the apparent owner, the holding bank is obligated to pay the funds to the real owner. As stated in Central National Bank of Baltimore v. Connecticut Mutual Life Insurance Company, 104 U. S. 54, 66, the question is always open

"To whom in equity does it (the funds) beneficially belong? If the money deposited belonged to a third person, and was held by the depositor in a fiduciary capacity, its character is not changed by being placed to his credit in his bank account."

The Continental Bank is under no liability to its customers for accepting the draft from the McCartney Bank for the collection items inasmuch as its contract with its customers permitted such course, and consequently is under no obligation to protect itself in that respect by attempting to seize the deposit account of the McCartney Bank. Regardless, however, of any liability in this respect on the part of the Continental Bank to its customers, the Continental Bank cannot appropriate on behalf of its customers the deposit of the McCartney Bank, now that the McCartney Bank is in receivership, inasmuch as such deposit is an asset of the receivership and belongs to all of the depositors and creditors of the McCartney Bank for pro rata distribution as required by law. To permit the offset would be not only a violation of the required rule of mutuality, but would be extending an unlawful preference to the customers of the Continental Bank (who are likewise creditors of the McCartney Bank) over the other depositors and creditors of the McCartney Bank.

The other matters referred to in the third point of respondent's brief do not require discussion.

We therefore ask that the judgment of the Circuit Court of Appeals for the Seventh Circuit be reversed.

Respectfully submitted,

AMOS C. MILLER,
SIDNEY S. GORHAM,
HENRY W. WALES,
EDWARD R. ADAMS,
    Counsel for Petitioner.

F. G. AWALT,
GEORGE P. BARSE,
JOHN F. ANDERSON,
GEORGE B. SPRINGSTON,
   Attorneys for Comptroller
    of the Currency,
       Of Counsel.

CPSIA information can be obtained
at www.ICGtesting.com
Printed in the USA
LVOW09s0303060318
568809LV00016B/1287/P

9 781270 234517